Letters From The Night Stalker

A Decade of Correspondence with Richard Ramirez

Marquis H.K.

Letters From The Night Stalker
A Decade of Correspondence with Richard Ramirez, by Marquis H.K.

Published by Dark Moon Press
P.O. Box 11496
Fort Wayne, Indiana 46858-1496
www.DarkMoonPress.com
DarkMoon@DarkMoonPress.com

ISBN-13: 9798668486335

© 2020 Dark Moon Press

No part of this book may be reproduced or transmitted in any form or by any means without written permission from author or publisher. All rights reserved. This book or any portion thereof may not be reproduced or used in any manner whatsoever without the express permission of the publisher except for the use of brief quotations in a book review or scholarly journal.

Table of Contents

Acknowledgements 7

Introduction 9

Chapter One 11

City Under Siege 11

Chapter Two 35

Research 35

Chapter Three 45

Correspondence 45

Chapter Four 73

Back In Touch 73

Gallery 118

About The Author 121

Other books by the Author 123

Acknowledgements

Richard Ramirez, the inspiration for this project, State Library of Queensland, Worldwide Online Printing Market Street Brisbane, Eric Vernor, Serial Killers, the Most Scary Abandoned Places Facebook page, Chad Morbid, Paul 'Stoney' Stone, Abbie Dexterous, Agni Kudra, Dan Boeren.

Contributors

Chad Morbid, Paul 'Stoney' Stone, Dan Boeren

Front Cover Design and Artwork

Chad Morbid – Morbid Art

Back Cover Design and Artwork

Paul 'Stoney' Stone – OTP Graphics

Introduction

I've always been intrigued by serial killers and I'm certainly not alone here. There are many people who share this morbid fascination. There is something about their psyche that compels and repels us in equal measure. Indeed, society breeds them, whether it be through childhood resentment or years of pent-up anger due to social alienation, we read their stories and feel somehow connected to them. Often, on the exterior, they are just like you and me: living in a suburban street, working a day-to-day job, some even have families.

Richard Ramirez struck a chord with me, as he was none of these things and didn't pretend to be. He projected himself as society's worst nightmare, embracing all the stereotypical cliches, a self-proclaimed devil worshipper fuelled by heavy metal music and narcotics. He was the real boogeyman that scared you as a kid, creeping through your window on a mission from the Devil to unleash hell and sinister slaughter. Yet, he was also a very charismatic individual who put on a good show and remained defiant till the end at his trial. And whilst I certainly don't condone his actions, there's no denying the man certainly had a sense of character.

What follows is a personal account of my decade long acquaintance, experience and, indeed, friendship with one of the most notorious, reviled serial killers in history. Receiving letters directly from his cell on San Quentin's Death Row where he resided for over two decades awaiting execution. We remained in contact right up until his death by natural causes on June 13, 2013, and we'd still be in contact now if he was still alive. Since his passing, I thought it was time that I shared my experiences with this evil, yet interesting, individual. Included is a collection of personal letters, artwork and newspaper clippings I accumulated over the years. I must point out that this is not in any way meant to be a biography of the man or his crimes. I've touched base on that for introductory purposes only but that's it. For that I strongly recommend *The Night Stalker – The Life and Crimes of Richard Ramirez* by Philip Carlo mentioned within these pages. I hope this proves as interesting and fascinating a read for you as it was for me corresponding with the man.

- Marquis H.K.

Chapter One

City Under Siege

The year is 1985, the city of Los Angeles is in the grip of fear from an elusive killer. He comes at night, choosing houses at random, stealthily creeping in through unlocked doors and windows. Brutally stabbing, shooting, raping and robbing his victims. He seems to have no set pattern. Different weapons are used at each crime scene; handguns, knives, machetes, tire irons and hammers, sometimes he restrains his victims using thumbcuffs, other times he uses electrical tape to bind and torture his victims. Making them 'Swear to Satan' and say they 'Love Satan' before ransacking and robbing the premises. The only calling cards he leaves is Satanic pentagrams scrawled on the walls and on some of the victims' bodies. It's also one of the hottest summers on record forcing residents to lock their doors and bolt their windows shut despite the heat. Sales of guns and home security systems skyrocket. The killer is like a shark in a feeding frenzy. There have been five attacks in little more than a week. It seems no one is safe from who the press had dubbed as the 'Night Stalker.' He meticulously follows the media coverage of himself. Even boldly telling some survivors to 'Tell them the Night

Stalker was here'

The Night Stalker murder spree left thirteen people dead and went from June 1984 to August 1985. He was very meticulous in covering his tracks, always wearing gloves to avoid leaving fingerprints. The only leads police had to go on were composite drawings from some of the surviving victims, a baseball cap of the rock band AC/DC found at one of the first murder sites and a footprint of an Avia sneaker.

On August 18, 1985 he took his murderous urge north to the city of San Francisco. He entered the residence of 62-year-old Peter Pan and shot him and his wife Barbara before scrawling a pentagram and the phrase 'Jack The Knife' on the wall with red lipstick. The then Mayor of San Francisco, Dianne Feinstein, gave a televised press conference informing the public of the leads that the police had to go on, including the Avia footprint. This infuriated the Los Angeles detectives working on the case since they knew the killer followed the media coverage of himself; unbeknownst to her, he was watching the press conference. He promptly dumped the sneakers over the side of the Golden Gate Bridge. The big break came on August 24, 1985 when he struck a residence in Mission Viejo. He drove around the streets with the headlights turned off when he was spotted by a thirteen-year-old boy fixing his motor scooter in the driveway, there was something about the driver that spooked him, he looked creepy and malevolent. The stalker then proceeded to the residence of Bill Carns and his 27-year-old fiancé. He shot Bill three times in the head before raping and sodomising his fiancé.

Announcing that he was the Night Stalker and making her swear to Satan before making off with some jewellery and $400 cash. The couple survived. The kid fixing his scooter looked up and saw the 'weird looking guy' in black drive by again. The Night Stalker case had everyone on edge, so he made sure this time to try and write down the licence plate number and he managed to get the last three digits. The Stalker got back on the freeway and headed to downtown Los Angeles. He normally kept his gloves on whilst driving but the night was hot and his hands were sweating, so he removed them. He dumped the stolen orange Toyota in a shopping centre car park, making sure to carefully wipe down the steering wheel, shift and rear-view mirror of all prints, however, he missed one fingerprint on the outside of the mirror which he'd adjusted earlier. It was a combination of things which marked the beginning of the end for the elusive Stalker. When word reached the kid who was fixing his scooter of the Carns attack just a few streets away, he immediately told his parents who then notified the Orange County police, who in turn notified detectives Gil Carrillo and Frank Salerno, the leads the Night Stalker task force. They visited the crime scene in Mission Viejo and were convinced their man was back in Los Angeles. A man by the name of Jesse Perez also contacted Carrillo and Salerno stating that he was sure who the Night Stalker was. Salerno spoke of an acquaintance who he knew from the Los Angeles Greyhound bus terminal by the name of 'Rick' who was from El Paso. He was a professional burglar, wore black and was always talking about Satan as the supreme being.

Every cop in the city was also looking for the orange Toyota which was used in the Carns attack. Police located it at the shopping centre, exactly where the Stalker had left it. They staked it out, hoping he would return, but he never did. It was taken to the Orange County Sheriff's garage lab where technicians went over it hoping to find a print. They were just about to throw it in when a female technician discovered the print on the rearview mirror. The cops interviewed more acquaintances of Rick and discovered his last name was Ramirez. The next job was to try and match the print with all the Rick, Ricardo and Richard Ramirezes on file. It was run through a computer and it matched the name of Richard Munoz Ramirez, a tall, lanky El Paso drifter. He had a record for petty crimes including theft and dealing drugs. His mug shot was shown to Jesse Perez, who verified that it was indeed the 'Rick' that he knew.

The police reluctantly released the photo to the press taking the gamble that it could tip the Stalker off who in turn could disappear. The next day his photo was on the front page of every newspaper in California as the prime suspect in the Night Stalker case. His name was also the first word spoken from every newscaster on every channel.

The next day cops were dispatched to the Los Angeles Greyhound bus terminal on the very real possibility that the Stalker had gotten word they were on to him and attempted to flee. They had no idea he was on his way into L.A., therefore didn't take any notice of inbound buses. He had been to Tuscan, Arizona to visit his brother who wasn't in so decided to return. It seems the only person in the city that didn't know everyone was looking for Richard Ramirez was him!

He went to a nearby grocery store to get himself a Pepsi and noticed elderly Mexican women staring at him, pointing muttering 'El Matador' (The Killer). He looked down and saw his own face staring back at him from the front page of Spanish newspaper, *La Opinion*. He grabbed a copy and fled. The owner was instantly on the phone to the police. That's it, they were on to him. Everywhere he went people were recognising him. He hopped on a bus where people had copies of newspapers pointing him out. He could hear police sirens and knew they were coming for him. Police helicopters were also dispatched. He ran like a gazelle across busy roads, through people's yards, effortlessly vaulting six-foot-high fences. His last thought was to steal a car and drive over the border to Mexico. People in the neighbourhood, on their porches were recognising him and called the police. Three teenage boys began to follow him until he told them to 'Get the fuck away from me!'

He headed into Hubbard Street in East Los Angeles. He attempted to steal a woman's car but her husband and her two sons came to her aid by whacking Richard in the head with a two foot iron bar. He got out and began to run down Hubbard Street with an angry mob in pursuit with bats and clubs. Cries of 'El Matador!' echoed up and down the block. A metal bar hissed through the air striking Richard on the head, knocking him to the ground. The crowd stood over he heard of them say, 'Go ahead, get up man and you're fucking dead.' LAPD cruisers arrived on the scene. Funny enough the first on the scene was a deputy who shared his name – Andres Ramirez.

'What's your name?' asked Deputy Ramirez.

'Ricardo Ramirez,' answered Richard, who was bleeding from the wound.

They bandaged his head and put him in the back of the car.

The Night Stalker's reign of terror was over.

Richard Leyva Munoz Ramirez was born on February 29, 1969, the youngest of Julian and Mercedes Ramirez. His father was a strict disciplinarian with a bad temper, just like his father had been. To escape his violent outbursts, Richard would often sleep in the local cemetery.

As a twelve-year-old he was heavily influenced by his older cousin, Miguel (Mike), who adopted the young Richard as his protégé. Mike was a decorated U.S. Army Green Beret combat veteran who had done a stint in Vietnam. He'd show him polaroid photographs including, Vietnamese women he'd raped and even on where Mike posed with a severed head. It was war and they were the enemy, so no one cared. He taught Richard how to kill with stealth and surety, how to effectively creep up on someone with a gun and knife. The turning point came when he witnessed Mike shoot his wife, Jessie, at point blank range with a .38 calibre revolver during a domestic argument. He warned her that if she didn't stop nagging him and 'put a lid on it,' he would shoot her and he did. The seeds were sown.

Mike was found not guilty of Jessie's murder by reason of insanity (his combat record as a mitigating factor). He was released in 1977 after four years' incarceration at the Texas State Mental Hospital. His influence over Richard continued. Happy days were here again as they resumed cruising and doing drugs together.

Whilst still in high school, the adolescent Richard took a job at a local Holiday Inn. His violent sexual fantasies began to well and truly manifest. He used his passkey to rob patrons and his employment was abruptly cut short when a guest returned to his room to find Richard attempting to rape his wife. Though he gave Richard a flogging, criminal charges were dropped when the couple who lived out of state declined to return to testify against him.

At the age of 22 he moved to California where he settled permanently. It's also here where he developed a serious interest in Satanism and heavy metal music. His all-time favourite band was Australian rock band AC/DC. He listened to the album *Highway To Hell* repeatedly. In particular the song 'Night Prowler; struck a chord with him; the song is about a prowler entering sleeping womens' bedrooms, which is exactly what he did. The band themselves ridiculed the association and the publicity from the Night Stalker case that resulted in the cancellation of some of their concerts. Some religious hysterics even stating that

AC/DC was an acronym for 'Anti- Christ Devil Child.'

Singer Brian Johnson couldn't believe anyone took the bands lyrics seriously; 'I can't believe with what some people come up with. I've even heard there is some sort of Devil worship in the band. It's so silly.' Guitarist Malcolm Young also stated, 'Why are all these bible belt people ranting and raving about us? *Highway To Hell* is about life on the road.'

The jury selection for the trial started on July 22, 1988. The trial would take years; Richard's lawyers kept delaying it. He was charged with thirteen counts of murder and forty other counts of rape and assault. He used this time to work on his persona and image. He put on a good show for the cameras, flashing a pentagram he had drawn on his hand and yelling 'Hail Satan!' He also attracted a horde of young female groupies who were mesmerised by his looks and mystique. He grew his hair and, indeed, looked more like a rock star than someone on trial for multiple murders: like a cross between Jim Morrison and Paul Stanley from KISS. He also had a defiant rebellious attitude; staring people down in court. The court had to endure the gory details of some of the horrors committed, including one of the victims eyeballs removed.

Throughout his trial, he was incarcerated at the Los Angeles County Jail. Actor Sean Penn was also serving a 60-day sentence for assaulting a photographer, he even stayed a couple of cells down from Richard. He gave a note to a guard requesting Penn's autograph. Penn wrote back –

'Dear Richard, whilst incarcerated, it's impossible not to feel a kinship with you fellow inmates. Well, Richard, it appears I've achieved the impossible. I feel absolutely no kinship with you' – Sean Penn.

Richard wrote back – 'Dear Sean, take care and hit 'em again' – Richard Ramirez 666.

Penn was married to Madonna at the time. Whilst visiting Penn, she asked, 'Who's the good-looking guy?'

He gave her a sly smirk, 'That 'good looking guy' is the Night Stalker! Wanna

meet him?'

'That guy gives me the shivers, but sure I'll meet him.'

'No way!' he retorted.

In a strange twist of fate one of the jurors, Phyllis Singletary, failed to show up for court one day. She was later found dead of a gunshot wound in her apartment. This terrified the rest of the jurors. They couldn't help wondering if Richard had somehow directed this from his prison cell or if it was the work of Satan himself. However, it was the result of neither. She had been shot by her boyfriend who later killed himself with the same weapon.

On September 20, 1989 he was found guilty and convicted of 13 counts of murder, 5 attempted murders, 11 sexual assaults and 14 burglaries. On November 7, 1989 Judge Michael Tynan sentenced him to death in San Quentin's gas chamber. However, he had one more performance; it was time to address the court.

BRUCE GUTHRIE in Los Angeles looks at the summer a city ran scared.

The man who had a city living in fear

FOR much of last summer the people of this city ran scared of one of LA's more infamous killers — the Nightstalker.

They bought weapons, locks and in many cases refused to leave homes that became prisons for them as the killer wandered and struck apparently at random.

RAMIREZ . . . caught after 14 killings.

Fourteen people had died when on August 30 last year East Los Angeles residents chased and captured a 26-year-old drifter from El Paso, who matched a photograph released the previous day by police.

With Richard Ramirez behind bars the killing stopped and the fear subsided. This week a new chapter in the grisly story was written when Ramirez was finally sent for trial on the murders.

"It appears to the court that the offences have been committed and there is sufficient cause to believe the defendant is guilty," LA municipal judge James Nelson said.

So ended a 29-day preliminary hearing that had heard some appalling accounts of The Nightstalker's killings.

Ramirez, who attracted a fan club of young girls during the hearing, was sent for trial on 14 murder counts, five counts of attempted murder, four rapes, three acts of oral copulation and four acts of sodomy.

Eighteen other counts, involving alleged sexual molesting of three young boys and girls, were dropped at the request of the prosecution. They had been fearful of the effects of public testimony on young victims.

Ramirez appeared quite ebullient through all this. As Judge Nelson read each of the charges, the accused killer smiled and chatted amiably with his defence counsel.

Later the accused Nightstalker was to say, through attorney Arturo Hernandez, that he believed there was "a lot of politics involved with the decision of the judge".

Judge Nelson, Ramirez apparently believed, was unwilling to take the heat that would ensue from any dismissal of charges against him.

The prosecution built its case on eyewitness identification and 84 pieces of stolen property from eight crime scenes.

Testimony during the preliminary hearing was always disturbing and often ghastly.

The court heard how some victims were shot, others stabbed and slashed and others beaten with claw hammers and tyre irons.

Ramirez, it was alleged, had murdered one elderly woman and then gouged out her eyes.

The most poignant moments came with the testimony of the six victims who survived Nightstalker attacks.

One of these was a frail Pakistani woman who identified Ramirez as her attacker, and then told the court he'd killed her husband before raping her.

"Near collapse in the courtroom," the woman said Ramirez had ordered her to "swear upon Satan" that she would not scream when he raped her.

"Oh God, I'm not going to scream," the woman told her attacker.

"Don't swear upon God, swear upon Satan," the woman testified her attacker told her.

Within days of Judge Nelson ordering Ramirez to stand trial for the Nightstalker killings, the case took another sensational turn.

According to previously unreleased transcripts, Ramirez admitted to police soon after his capture that he had killed the 14 victims.

LAPD officer Daniel Rodriguez told the preliminary hearing into the murders that Ramirez shouted through the window of a police car: "It's me, it's me."

"He then looked in a downward direction," Rodriguez testified, "and he kind of leaned over towards his knees and stated: 'I am glad you got me.'"

The police testimony had been made in camera during the 29-day preliminary hearing, but it was made public after the judge had committed Ramirez for trial.

According to another LAPD officer, George Thomas, Ramirez admitted he was the Nightstalker during an interview at police headquarters.

"I did it, you know. You guys got me, the Stalker," Rodriguez claimed the accused killer said.

"Then he (Ramirez) stated: 'Hey, I want a gun to play with. Russian roulette. I'd rather die than spend the rest of my life in prison.'"

Later, Thomas said, Ramirez started humming the Australian rock group AC/DC's *Night Prowler* and banged his head on a table as the police looked on.

The song includes the lyric: "Was that a noise outside the window? What's that shadow on the blind? As you lie there naked like a body in a tomb, suspended animation as I slip into your room. I'm your night prowler."

The damning testimony was apparently held back initially because Judge Nelson thought it might prejudice a fair trial for the accused. Ramirez' lawyers denied their client had ever said he was the killer.

'You don't understand me. You are not expected to. You are not capable. I am beyond your experience. I am beyond good and evil. I will be avenged. Lucifer dwells in all of us. I don't know why I'm even wasting my breath, but what the hell? For what is said of my life, there have been lies in the past and there will be lies in the future. I don't believe in the hypocritical, moralistic dogma of this so-called civilised society. I need not look beyond this courtroom to see all the liars, the haters, the killers, the crooks, the paranoid cowards, truly the *Trematodes* of the earth.

'You maggots make me sick! Hypocrites, one and all. We are all expendable for a cause. No one knows that better than those who kill for policy, clandestinely or openly, as do the governments of the world which kill in the name of God and country . . . I don't need to hear all of society's rationalisations. I've heard them all

21

before . . . Legions of the night, nightbreed, repeat not the errors of the Night Prowler and show no mercy. That's it.'

When asked by a reporter how he felt about his death sentence he retorted, 'Big deal, death always went with the territory. See you in Disneyland.' He was flown by chopper to San Quentin's Death Row where he remained for the next twenty-three years. The trial cost $1.8 million which at the time made it the most expensive in the history of California. Only to be surpassed by the O.J. Simpson case in 1994.

He married one of his admirers and supporters, Doreen Lioy, on October 3, 1996. She wasn't like one of his younger groupies, she was a bit older and had led a somewhat sheltered life. The difference with Death Row weddings is that they omit the phrase 'Till death do us part' from the vows.

AC/DC's *Highway To Hell*, Richard Ramirez's favourite album, which he listened to repeatedly whilst stalking the streets of L.A.

The now iconic photo of Richard Ramirez flashing a pentagram in court

Article on Ramirez also featured Charles Manson and David Berkowitz The Son Of Sam who terrorised New York City in the mid 70's.

'Night Stalker' trial told of horror killings

SUSPECTED "Night Stalker" Richard Ramirez in a Los Angeles court yesterday as prosecutors outline charges against him.

LOS ANGELES.— A Texas drifter accused of being the "Night Stalker" gouged out the eyes of one of his victims, a prosecutor said yesterday.

Deputy District Attorney Philip Halpin, opening the trial of Richard Ramirez who is accused of brutally murdering 13 people, said Maxine Zazzara, 44, had also been shot twice and her throat had been cut.

The attack on the Zazzara home in Whittier, a Los Angeles suburb, occurred in March 1985.

Vincent Zazzara, 64, was found dead in his study with a bullet-wound in his head.

Ramirez, 28, wearing dark glasses and a pinstripe suit, jotted occasional notes as Halpin described the attack on Zazzara and her husband Vincent, and others attributed to the "Night Stalker".

It took Superior Court Judge Michael Tynan nearly 20 minutes to read the 43 felony charges against the lanky, long-haired defendant.

They include 13 murder counts, relating to killings between June 1984 and August 1986. Ramirez could face the death penalty if convicted.

Most of the victims were attacked at night in their homes, the male occupants often being shot before the woman was sexually assaulted.

A major part of the prosecution's case is expected to be a cache of jewellery stolen from the victims. *Reuter*

Article on Richard Ramirez's groupies who attended his trial.

In a strange twist of fate one of the Night Stalker jurors was murdered during the trial.

FRIDAY, SEPTEMBER 22, 1989

Guilty verdict for the 'Night Stalker'

LOS ANGELES.— The "Night Stalker", a killer who terrorised California with savage random attacks on people in their homes at night, was convicted yesterday of 13 murders.

Richard Ramirez, 29, a self-proclaimed devil worshipper who committed most of his murders and brutal sexual attacks in the summer of 1985, also was convicted of attempted murders, burglaries and sexual assaults by a Los Angeles Supreme Court jury.

A Superior Court jury now must decide whether Ramirez deserves to die in the gas chamber or face life in prison.

Ramirez, a Texas drifter, heard the verdict by closed-circuit television as he sat in his courtroom cell after refusing to wear leg shackles in the courtroom.

The Superior Court jury deliberated for 22 days before reaching its verdict in the six-month trial.

Witnesses at the trial told horror stories of husbands murdered by a single shot to the head and their wives raped after being ordered to "swear upon Satan".

Lawyers for Ramirez maintained he was a victim of mistaken identity but the jury found him guilty of all 13 murders.

Reuter

RICHARD Ramirez

Killer bound for 'Disneyland'

RICHARD Ramirez, the "Night Stalker" who butchered or raped more than a dozen people in an orgy of violence that terrorised southern California in 1985, was today sentenced to death in the gas chamber.

Superior Court Judge Michael Tynan followed the recommendation of the jury that convicted the devil-worshiping 29-year-old on September 20.

In the courtroom before his sentencing, Ramirez, (above), uttered a rambling, nearly inaudible statement that ended with the words: "Lucifer dwells within us all."

Ramirez, who entered unlocked houses at night to attack people in their beds, was convicted of 13 murders and 30 other felonies, including rape, burglary and sodomy.

The jurors, some of whom said the defendant had tried to intimidate them during the trial by sneering and glaring at them, recommended on October 4 that he be sentenced to death rather than life in prison.

A snarling, gravelly-voiced Ramirez had sneered at the possibility of being sentenced to death.

"Big deal. Death comes with the territory," he told reporters after the jury's recommendation. "See you in Disneyland."

After his conviction, Ramirez flashed a two-fingered "devil sign" at photographers and muttered, "Evil."

Judge sends unrepentant Night Stalker to chamber

LOS ANGELES.— The Night Stalker killer was on death row at San Quentin yesterday, unrepentant and vowing he would be avenged.

In a final statement to the Los Angeles Superior Court, Richard Ramirez — the self-proclaimed satanist found guilty of 13 murders — attacked the system that has condemned him to the gas chamber.

"You maggots make me sick, hypocrites one and all," he said.

The 29-year-old drifter from El Paso, Texas, was sentenced yesterday after being convicted last month of a series of burglaries, rapes, assaults, mutilations and murders that terrorised California in the summer of 1985.

Relatives of his victims have requested per-

RAMIREZ

mission to be present at the execution but they will have to be patient.

California has not used its gas chamber since 1967 and the appeals process for Ramirez is likely to last as long as seven years.

"Legions of the night, nightbreed, repeat not the errors of my father and show no mercy. I will be avenged. Lucifer dwells in us all," he told the court.

A survivor from one of his attacks, Christopher Petersen, said it was time for Ramirez to be held accountable for his actions. Petersen and his wife were attacked in their home. Petersen still has a bullet lodged in his head.

His wife Virginia said they were in constant pain from their injuries and could still hear the screams of "Mummy don't die" from her four-year-old daughter during the attack.

The judge said there were no mitigating factors. Ramirez had beaten, strangled, and stabbed his victims to death, usually breaking into their homes at night and shooting the male occupant before sexually assaulting the woman.
— DAN McDONNELL

Richard Ramirez's reaction to receiving the death sentence was 'Big deal, death always came with the territory. See you in Disneyland.'

Ramirez vowed that Satan would avenge his execution

Ramirez gives the Sign of the Horns after receiving nineteen death sentences

Richard Ramirez's mugshot was plastered on the front page of every California newspaper. The Spanish *La Opinion* is what greeted him in a grocery store which led to his capture.

Chapter Two

Research

I'd followed the Night Stalker trial as it was happening. I thought he was one out there dude, almost like a cult leader. A friend of mine showed me a magazine which featured his artwork. *ANSWER Me!* was an independent, self-published inflammatory magazine by husband and wife team, Jim and Debbie Goad. It was very nihilistic in nature and focused heavily on serial killers and other social pathologies. It ran from 1991 to 1994 and lasted only four issues. The fourth issue being the most controversial, known as the 'Rape Issue.' It featured a parody dating profile page of Richard Ramirez.

Sometime in the late 90's, Foxtel screened the 1989 T.V. movie *Manhunt – Search For The Night Stalker*, a factual, albeit tame drama based on the case. It was released just after Richard had been convicted and he was allowed to watch it from his prison cell. He evidently complained that the guy who portrayed him (Greg Cruz) looked nothing like him. This totally renewed my interest in the Night Stalker case.

I figured there had to be a decent book written on him somewhere. I went to the American Bookstore – a then import specialist in Brisbane. They advised me that there was one available *The Night Stalker – The Life and Crimes of Richard Ramirez* by Philip Carlo, published in 1996, which would cost $50 Australian. I ordered it straight away and it arrived around two weeks later. A thick hardback spanning 400+ pages, along with multiple photographs. This was going to be an interesting read and I couldn't wait to get my teeth into it. You also have to understand that I didn't have internet at this time, so all research had to be conducted in the old school manner. And if I was lucky enough, I'd catch the occasional documentary that was aired. He was the subject of an episode of *Great Crimes and Trials Of The 20th Century*, which aired in 1995 one late Sunday night on the ABC. I certainly wasn't disappointed with the book. I couldn't put the thing down; if you're looking for a proper biography, then look no further than this. I cannot recommend it enough. It is the definitive account and a true crime masterpiece. Painstakingly researched over three years based on over a hundred exclusive interviews with Richard from Death Row. From his first brushes with the law to his deadliest expeditions. It also interviews his family members and detailed accounts of his time spent with cousin Mike, who undoubtedly played a major role in who he came to be. It also documents the unprecedented police and civilian manhunt and the trial which was one of the most sensational in California history. An updated version was later published with an extra chapter on the Death Row wedding. Philip Carlo sadly passed away on November 8, 2010, aged 61.

It's fair to say that my renewed interest turned into somewhat of an obsession. I was in Brisbane's Rocking Horse Records where I spotted a vinyl LP by Seattle hardcore punk band that Zeke called *True Crime*. The cover featured Richard Ramirez giving the Satanic Sign of the Horns. I bought it on the spot for the cover alone. It also featured a bonus poster of the same image and is a killer album. It was released on Australian label Dropkick Records in 1999 and contains sixteen tracks of blistering hardcore punk dripping with attitude. Not unlike rock 'n' roll legends Motorhead, so winner all round!

As stated previously, I didn't have access to internet, so I found myself taking trips to the State Library every Sunday afternoon to print out newspaper articles. All the newspapers are on micro reel film and allocated by year. So to find what you're looking for, you have to know what year it took place, load the film to the machine and away you go. It is a lengthy process and requires patience, going through each newspaper page by page. Luckily, I remembered most of the articles from the 80's and had a good idea where they were so it didn't take me long. Besides, I didn't mind, I saw it as a leisurely productive afternoon out. I had all the articles I was looking for within two weeks, printed them out and keep them in a black folder.

In 1999, I caught a story on the morning *Today* show. It was on this guy by the name of Jason Moss from Las Vegas who'd written a book on his personal acquaintance with infamous serial killers called *The Last Victim*. He did it as a project for his university thesis. I instantly ordered a copy from the American Bookstore and found it a very compelling read. He developed a relationship with serial killer John Wayne Gacy. Gacy at the time was on Death Row for the murder of thirty-three teenage boys, most of their remains were found in the crawlspace under his Chicago home. Gacy was quite an upstanding member of the community, he ran his own construction business and hosted parties for children in hospital dressed as 'Pogo the Clown.' However, his favourite past time was restraining and torturing young boys.

Moss first began corresponding him by mail, posing as an introverted, lost, emotionally unstable middle-class white boy. This drew Gacy in, hook, line and sinker – perfect prey. The correspondence was quickly followed by phone calls, which Gacy made call-collect from Death Row. Followed by prison visits during which Moss was left alone with Gacy in his cell. Moss, being only eighteen at the time, was a prime candidate, and even though he was a kickboxer, weight lifter and much bigger and fitter than Gacy, the killer still managed to mentally overpower and intimidate him, even going as far as threatening to sexually assault him. When Moss broke contact, Gacy threatened to turn him over to the authorities for having an incestual relationship with his brother. Moss then revealed that what he portrayed to Gacy was all bullshit; that Gacy was just a project and he had been playing him all along for his university thesis. A disgruntled Gacy knew he had been had. He complained to his brother that Moss had taken him for a big ride. In effect, Moss had been his last victim before he was executed not long after by lethal injection in 1994. In a strange twist of fate, Moss also committed suicide. Of all the dates he chose June 6, 2006 – 6/6/6 to take his own life.

The book inspired a film, *Dear Mr Gacy* (2010) with William Forsythe playing the part of John Wayne Gacy.

Whilst undertaking research, Moss wrote and befriended other serial killers – Charles Manson, Jeffrey Dahmer and Richard Ramirez. Again, he adopted a false persona in accordance with the recipient. With Ramirez, he had read a copy of *The Satanic Bible* and portrayed himself as an avowed Satanist. Proclaiming allegiance to the Dark Lord and drawing pentagrams in red ink on the letters.

I thought to myself, well if he can do it, then so can I. It was time to have a crack at it myself.

Artwork and parody dating profile page as featured in *ANSWER Me!*

The NICE Stalker

Do you have what it takes to be Richard Ramirez's girlfriend?

Whatta hunk! Gorgeous teen idol Richard "the Night Stalker" Ramirez blows a kiss to his fans and promises, "I'll be out of jail soon!!"

Y'know, you're not a little girl anymore, at least it doesn't seem that way. Your boobs are full things on the front cover. Your breath smells worse, and those zits aren't quite as zany as they were at age seventeen.

And since you're now an adult woman, you're having rape fantasies almost nightly. Rape fantasies are not "crazy"; you're having rape fantasies almost nightly with that same sullen stranger; your legs spell at a 180° angle. Who do you imagine is your captor?

The Green Giant wears the tarnished you were a desk. But you're a probable rape and some little sixteen-year-olds are just doesn't cut it anymore. Leave the experienced stars to the chicken hawks. Open your eyes, close your eyes, and think about a MAN.

Richard Ramirez is a Guy who's been around the block a few times. They say he fucks women while killing them, so he just might know his way around a bedroom. And (we whisper), so do the girls we gaze over him!

A mutual friend sent an actual recipient introduced Ricky to us on... starring with our second issue. Some bad folks in the government turn to Ramirez looked at us, through prison people, but we don't believe them. Not our Ricky. He called Dickie "radical." Said we were "a match made in hell."

We love him.

But it gets lonely year after year without your death's bedmate, and Ricky's thoughts often turn to romance. Especially if it involves Chinese chicks who like more a problem. Since insane is a magazine about sexual killers—and NOTHING BUT serial killers—we feel compelled to find a girlfriend for one of our favorites.

Ricky, we are never enough to take time out from his busy schedule and answer a few questions through the mail. Ten questions. A very personal ten-question quiz. The answers are not necessarily RIGHT answers, and take a long gander at those you-like-his unflinching, authentic, NOTHING BUT actual answers. Then next time you're spaced gushing over sumo-chop photos. They next time you're spaced gushing over some hunky dreamboat who's really nothing more than a glob of hair gel, ask yourself this: How could we like this, for you?

☆ How has your life YOUR?
☆ How has your life changed as a result of your success?
☆ Privacy is a thing of the past.
☆ What's your message to your fans?
Keep your spirit strong.

☆ Do you prefer to be called Richard or Richie?
  What's in a name?
☆ Are you seeing anybody right now?
  No. Only in my dreams.
☆ What is something people would be surprised to know about you?
  That I'm a nice stalker.
☆ What kind of clothes do you like to wear?
  Jumpsuits with lots of pockets.
☆ Would you describe yourself as "self-crazy"?
  Yeah, but I don't have any time to write and date them. Not crazy. Just lazy.
☆ If you like a girl, how do you get her to notice you?
  I pull out my gun.
☆ How do you feel about being a teen heartthrob?
  Great. Keep the hate mail coming.
☆ What do you like to do for fun?
  Use drugs.
☆ What's the one thing you would change about the world if you could?
  No more politicians.
  Or, for that matter, government.
☆ What's one thing you'd change about yourself?
  Not a damn thing except what I'm at.

Richie answers the tough questions! Take a look—do HIS tastes match YOURS?

Move over, Joey Lawrence! Take a hike, Jonathan Brandis! Suck a dick, Macaulay Culkin! Only **Richard Ramirez** gives the girls what they deserve!

Name: Richard Ramirez
Birth Date: 2-28-60
Birthplace: Texas
Current Residence: Box E37101 San Quentin, CA 94974
Height: 6'1"
Weight: 180 lbs
Hair Color: Black
Eye Color: Red

Favorite Sports: Rugby, Football, Boxing
Favorite Music: Heavy Metal
Favorite Actress: Samantha Strong
Favorite Vacation Spot: URANUS
Favorite Food: Women's feet
Favorite Color: Red
Pastimes/Hobbies: traveling and measuring coffins
Biggest Like: Cocaine
Biggest Dislikes: Hypocrites, Authority
Make a wish: To have my finger on a nuclear trigger device
What do you look for in a girl? Nice ass, Good legs.
Perfect way to spend a date: Moonlit night drinking rum at a cemetery
Describe yourself: Asshole - and proud of it.
Motto: Live each day as if it's your last

41

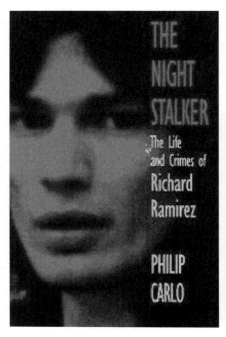 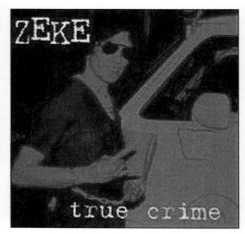

The Night Stalker – The Life and Crimes of Richard Ramirez by Philip Carlo

True Crime by Seattle hardcore punk band Zeke featured Richard Ramirez on the cover giving the Satanic Sign of the Horns. *The Last Victim* by Jason Moss served as an inspiration for my correspondence. *Manhunt – Search For The Night Stalker*; TV movie – 1989

 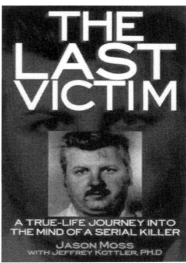

Greg Cruz as Richard Ramirez in *Manhunt*

Richard with author Philip Carlo in San Quentin

Chapter Three

Correspondence

So, I made a few enquiries and a source, that for some reason now totally escapes me gave me the telephone number for the California Inmate Location.

I called them, 'Hello , I'm calling from Australia.'

'Talk, I love your accent.' The female operator responded.

'You may be able to help me, I'm looking for the postal address of Richard Ramirez, AKA the Night Stalker.'

'Well Sir, to locate him I'll need his date of birth. Just a quick search now and I'm already on my fourth page of Richard Ramirez's.'

'Okay, will call you back.' I checked in Carlo's book for his date of birth, which was February 28, 1960.

'Hi, I called a few minutes ago.'

'Oh yeah, Richard Ramirez.'

'That's right, well his date of birth is February 28, 1960.'

Whilst she was searching, I asked her if she remembered the Night Stalker case. She recalled that it was in L.A.

'Okay, you got a pen?'

'Yeah, fire away.'

'You need to write to – Richard Ramirez E37101, San Quentin State Prison, San Quentin, California, 94964, USA.'

'Thanks, you've been a great help.'

'Are you really calling from Australia?'

'Yeah.'

Why are you looking for this person?'

'I'm just interested in corresponding with him.'

'Fair enough, my pleasure.'

'Bye.'

'Bye.'

The next step was to figure out how I was going to word the letter to get a guaranteed response. I know he got a ton of mail, especially from women, so it was important to write it in such a way to get his interest. I'd been into Satanism for a while and definitely considered myself a Satanist. Though, I didn't officially join up with the Church of Satan until 2003. I'd read all of Anton Lavey's books and the philosophy really struck a chord with me. In the sense that it is an epicurean, individualistic philosophy based on rational self-interest. With life being the ultimate indulgence and the real fire of Satan burns within oneself. Satanists see themselves as being their own gods. I'd read *The Satanic Bible* years prior and it instantly clicked with me. This had been me all along. After the bullshit Jason Moss fed him just for his project, I thought it was important to convince him that I was the real deal.

So, I started off by introducing myself and letting him know I'd been following his case since the 80's. Told him a little bit about myself and my then girlfriend at the time who went by the name of Devilla. I also informed him that if there was anything else he'd like to know about us or Australia, then I'd be happy to share what I could. I was also involved heavily in the local underground music scene at the time, promoting bands and hosting Goth/Metal Clubs. So, I included some photos from club nights and a couple of gig flyers. To be certain that he received it,

I sent it by international registered post, that way, someone at San Quentin would have to sign for it. Now, it was just a matter of waiting and hoping for the best. The letter would take around ten days, give or take a couple to arrive.

Of all the serial killers, Ramirez was the only one I was interested in corresponding with. He was also one of the last ones still alive; Bundy and Gacy had been executed and Dahmer had been murdered in prison by a fellow inmate. I had no interest in interacting with Bundy and Gacy anyway. Dahmer was in introverted homosexual with no real character. Charlie Manson did interest me to a certain degree, but his replies would have been incoherent mumbo jumbo. The only other one that was of interest to me was David Berkowitz – The Son Of Sam. I'd read *The Ultimate Evil* by Maury Terry, which scrutinizes the theory that Berkowitz didn't act alone; that he was a part of a Satanic Death Cult that held sinister meetings and rituals in New York's Untermyer Park. I called Attica Prison, where Berkowitz used to be housed, but they informed me he'd been moved to Sullivan Correctional Centre, South Fallsburg, New York State. They gave me the address and I wrote but never heard back. This didn't surprise me, as he was now a born-again Christian going by the name 'The Son Of Hope.' So, I'm guessing he wasn't about to answer my questions about Satanic rituals in Untermyer and the Death Cult.

Richard and I also shared some mutual interests. We both loved heavy metal music, horror movies, hot chicks and had an interest in serial killers and historical tyrants, and of course Satanism. Though what really struck me about Richard was his charisma. I was at work one afternoon when my girlfriend called. We were living in the Brisbane western suburb of Chelmer. I had an afternoon/early evening job cleaning a kitchen up the road in Graceville. I asked her to check that day's mail since I just had this feeling, she did so, reluctantly, and was going through them. And there it was, she shrieked with excitement – 'WE'VE GOT A LETTER FROM RICHARD RAMIREZ!!!!' She read it out but I just couldn't wait to get home to see it for myself. I was going by the pseudonym 'Marceese' back then. It's just something I made up as a DJ name. I just thought it sounded kinda demonic, so I also used it as a literary name. His handwriting was what's known as 'Doctor's Writing,' so named because when a doctor writes out a script it's very small and barely legible, but I could make it out. It was addressed to Marceese/Devilla, he thanked us for the letter and what followed was a series of questions – Have you lived in Australia all your lives? So, both of you are DJ's? You must have a vast collection of records. What's life like for you? He complimented my t-shirt from the photo I sent him; it was a shirt of Satanic rock band, the Electric Hellfire Club, they used an inverted pentagram with goat's head as their logo. He wished he could wear one like it. He then went on to say, 'As for me, I live in a 6ft x 4ft cell, I've been locked up for fifteen years. I read, write, draw, sleep and watch TV. Life is life. He also asked if I write to 'others.' No doubt meaning other serial killers. He finished with, 'If you go to the beach there, and I'm sure you do, it would be great if you could get some photos of the females for me. Write back when you can. Take It E/Z –

Rick.' He also said to say hello to our friends in the photos we sent him. I couldn't believe it, I was ecstatic. I didn't have to wait long for a reply either. Around two weeks, I must have read the thing around fifty times. I wrote a reply that very evening. I rang San Quentin and asked if music tapes were permitted, they told me they weren't. Neither were magazines or books. The only things permitted were printed documents, handwritten letters and photographs. I was going to put a metal compilation together of bands I think he'd like. He had a squad that went through his mail before he received it. Anything deemed unacceptable would be returned. Later on, San Quentin would crack down on what inmates were allowed to receive, but I'll get to that later.

I asked him what bands he liked these days. I knew he loved AC/DC, but did he listen to the likes of Slayer or any death metal. Shock rockers like Marilyn Manson were also at the peak of their career then, so I asked what he thought of them and their gimmick. Particularly, their stage names, a juxtaposition combining that of a glamorous famous female celebrity with an infamous serial killer – Madonna Wayne Gacy, Daisy Berkowitz, Sara Lee Lucas and his own namesake, Twiggy Ramirez. I told him we'd recently seen them headlining the 1999 Big Day Out festival touring *Mechanical Animals* album. And that conservative Christian Minister/Politician, Fred Nile, tried to prevent them from entering the country due to singer Manson's association with the Church of Satan. I told him I didn't go to the beach, at least not in summer. I love the ocean and chicks in bikinis, but I have fair skin and fry in the harsh Australian sun; but I could still send photos of chicks in bikinis, no problem. So, I just cut a couple of pictures out of holiday brochures and sent them along with a couple of flyers in the envelope. Again, I sent it international registered post.

I had to wait a little longer this time for a reply, but the wait was well worth it. He enclosed a signed photo of himself, on the back was written – To Marceese and Devilla, Hail Satan! Richard Ramirez, Night Stalker. He also sent a piece of artwork done with multi-coloured ink. It looked like a tribal design, but it was made up of evil demonic looking faces. This was cool! On the back was written 'A Gift.' He apologised for the delayed response as he'd been ill. He also stated that he still liked AC/DC, as well as Black Sabbath, Metallica and Iron Maiden. Pink Floyd's *Dark Side Of The Moon* was also one of his favourites. He said he'd seen Marilyn Manson on TV and liked what he heard, same with Slayer. He also liked the girlie pics I'd sent him and asked to send more, no problem. He also asked if my faith (in Satanism) was strong. I wrote back and told him that I thought my faith was strong enough and that I did rituals when the need arose. I celebrated my 32nd birthday that year and sent him photos of the gathering I held at my front verandah playing pool. I knew he'd been a good pool player when free, so I asked him about it. He wrote back wishing me a happy belated birthday and that he'd been playing pool and billiards since he was a teenager. I'd also told him that I was a first dan black belt in Tae Kwon Do which got his interest since he too had studied various forms of martial arts and hand to hand combat; including boxing, Hapkido, Judo and wrestling. He was the only one with a decent sized yard as a kid, so him and his friends used it as a training ground. He was a big fan of Bruce Lee and Steven Seagal and informed me that Lee died whilst filming *Game Of Death*, and that they had to get another actor to fill in the scenes. There was no CGI back then, so the only option was disguise which didn't work too well.

I recall writing him Christmas Day of 1999. It was stinking hot and humid. I told him I was drinking an ice-cold Heineken as I was writing. Heineken had brought out promo 500 ml Millennium cans to celebrate the new Millennium. He asked if I'd read Philip Carlo's book on him, to which I replied that indeed I had and sent him the slipcover along with the poster in the Zeke record album for him to sign. He signed and returned both asking if I drank lots of Heineken. Adding that he really didn't drink much when free but had drank Heineken on a couple of occasions and liked it. I also discussed the possibility of visiting him one day. He liked the idea and said he'd have to send visit forms.

2000 was to be a busy year. I was managing, promoting and touring a lot of bands, both local and interstate. I'd tell all the bands of my correspondence with him, which they found interesting. I'd also send him photos, flyers and posters from the events. I got him to sign one of the band's posters – Psi-Kore; a Sydney band who we were good mates with.

Myself and Devilla had spent a weekend down the Gold Coast. There was this cool little short-lived shop down there that sold cool sinister shirts. I purchased an Anton Lavey shirt and ordered a Night Stalker shirt from their catalogue. We were browsing in one of those trashy tourist novelty stores in Surfers Paradise when we came across a postcard. It was a chick in a bikini that, when scratched, would reveal her nude body. We thought it would make an awesome gift for him so I purchased and sent with next letter. I also told him about the lunar eclipse we watched on the beach that night; it was the middle of winter so best time to visit the beach. I wanted to check out a store I knew existed called Wizard's Realm. It was a specialist store that sold all kinds of occult paraphernalia and ritual tools: candles, cauldrons, ritual daggers, incense, swords and spell books were among some of the items sold. They also had an authentic recording of Aleister Crowley. But it was just my luck that it happened to be Sunday and was closed.

He loved the scratch bikini card I sent him, he also sent more artwork of the Grim Reaper and Devil's Head. I thanked him for the piece he sent with the previous letter and said he used to do them bigger and better until his art supplies got yanked. He asked about our trip to the Gold Coast, adding the lunar eclipses are cool. Of course, he also asked about chicks in bikinis but I explained being the middle of *winter* there weren't that many. Maybe a couple, Devilla was also a very jealous type who hated me looking at other women. So, I couldn't exactly look out for them and get photos.

As previously stated, it was a very busy year for promoting tours and album launches at clubs. I'd book the bigger bands at Brisbane's

Waterloo Hotel in Newstead. I also did a lot of work with movie distribution companies promoting new releases – Roadshow, Paramount, Sony, 20th Century Fox. Mainly horror and films of a dark nature. They'd give me promo passes as giveaways along with posters and flyers and they'd provide key artwork for the movies to be included on posters and ads in street press magazines. Any leftover promo materials I'd send to Rick. We talked a lot about movies. The Julian Temple Sex Pistols documentary *The Filth and the Fury* had just been released. He said he quite liked the Sex Pistols but didn't know there was a movie on them. He told me of a French guy, Nico Claux, dubbed 'The Vampire of Paris,' who also wrote to him. Claux is a former morgue attendant and grave robber who spent seven years in prison for killing a homosexual. Whilst working at the morgue, he would allegedly eat strips of muscles from the bodies, even taking them home to cook them. He had another job at a hospital where he claimed to have stolen blood bags, put them in his fridge, mix with human ash and drink them. Though he was never put on trial or convicted for any of these acts so some argue that they are a product of his imagination to boost his macabre profile. It seems to work for him as it gets him appearances on talk shows, interviews on documentaries and magazines; which in turn helps with the sales of his serial killer paintings. Rick sent me samples of his artwork, which included himself and Anton Lavey.

Another notorious serial killer housed on San Quentin's Death Row was Lawrence Bittaker. He and his accomplice, Ray Norris, were known as the 'Toolbox Killers,' due to the fact they tortured their victims with pliers and ice picks. Together they kidnapped, raped, tortured and murdered five teenage girls over a period of five months in Southern California in 1979. They would cruise around in a windowless van looking for victims to abduct. They even recorded them torturing their last victim, which was played in court at Bittaker's trial. It sickened both the prosecution and the jury, many of whom made a dash for the exit to be physically sick. Bittaker and Norris featured in the 1982 documentary *The Killing Of America*. I asked Rick if he was still there. He replied that he was but real old. Bittaker resides there to this day.

I also asked Rick if he knew of notorious punk singer GG Allin and if German Satanic vampire murderer, Manuela Ruda, had corresponded with him. He replied that he knew of GG Allin and wrote to his brother, Merle, who Rick described as a mellow guy. I asked if he knew of Australia's most notorious serial killer, Ivan Milat – the Backpacker Killer. He said he hadn't and asked about him, adding that he thought Australia's most infamous killer was that 'Mark guy who shot all those tourists.' He was referring to Martin Bryant and the 1996 Port Arthur Massacre in 1996 where 35 people were shot dead. We also discussed the Columbine High School Shootings saying that it made big news there. He did recall an incident during his trial where Anton Lavey's daughter, Zeena, and her husband, Nikolas Schreck, attended. They had a magical school at the time called the Werewolf Order. There were twelve of them and when they walked in heads turned. As they were all wearing long black trench coats and sat down at the same time! Both Nikolas and Zeena are now Tantric Buddhist religious teachers. By this stage I felt that I'd gotten to know the guy well enough through mail correspondence, so I thought I'd try my luck with a phone call. I called San Quentin and the officer on the line told me that Richard Ramirez was currently a Grade A Death Row inmate, therefore did have phone privileges. I wrote him to try and set up a phone call, but he wrote back saying he didn't use the phone there. Maybe he just wasn't a phone person, who knows? I asked him about his female admirers who flocked to his trial in droves and visited him in prison. He stated that he didn't get visitors, only his wife twice a week behind glass. I guess the whole 'rock star status' had well and truly died off by now. He did say that his family kept in touch by mail, particularly his sister, Ruth, but rarely visited as they lived in other parts of the country.

He couldn't comprehend why Catholics and Protestants had such opposing beliefs when they were supposedly both Christian. I explained that they both worship the same god but have different belief systems. The location where it was most volatile in years gone by was Northern Ireland. But the situation there was more political than religious, with the Catholics wanting a united Ireland like the rest of the country, and the Protestants wanting to stay under British rule.

September 2000 saw the country in the grip of Olympic fever. As Sydney was host to the 2000 Olympics. He did ask me about this, as he did enjoy sport. Particularly contact sports – boxing, American Football, rugby, wrestling and any form of martial arts. I told him that I thought Sydney was a good host and was impressed by the opening ceremony.

The Creatures featuring Siouxsie Sioux and Budgie from Siouxsie and the Banshees also toured that month. They did an encore of Banshees songs. I wasn't sure if he was familiar with them, but I told him about it regardless as he always asked about concerts we attended. He told me the first concert he attended was Black Sabbath.

October saw The Cure headlining the now defunct Brisbane Livid Festival. They had recently released their *Blood Flowers* album and it was rumoured to be their last tour, which certainly wasn't the case. He'd seen them on TV and thought they were okay. A week later we were in Canberra for the annual Metal For The Brain festival. This was a charity event that ran for fifteen years. It was also Australia's largest metal festival at the time. It all started in 1990 when Canberra metal fan, Alec Hurley, was attempting to stop a fight outside a Canberra club. He in turn was set upon and left severely brain damaged. The following year his friends in the black metal thrash band, Armoured Angel, organised the first fundraiser featuring six bands. The festival grew from there and now featured over thirty acts from all over the country with diverse styles: thrash, death, black, industrial, hardcore and doom. It was basically a festival of heavy music and people came from all over Australia for the event.

On the way to Canberra, we stopped in Sydney for the night. We were trying to get US theatrical shock rock band, the Genitorturers, to Australia and had a meeting with one of their representatives and a Sydney promoter. We took the train to Canberra the next day. I wore my Night Stalker shirt to the festival and got a lot of comments from people who I struck up conversations with. I told how I was penpals with him and got some very interesting mixed reactions!

Rick told me he was receiving letters from other Australians and that he would put them in touch with us. Devilla said it was a result of me 'shooting my mouth off at Metal For The Brain.' I ridiculed this, saying people were there for the bands and being an all day event had consumed more than enough alcohol that they'd barely remember. A couple of people did get in touch though. One girl from Sydney contacted me via email by the name of Dee and one from a girl named Deanne via a letter in the mail. It was only a short letter, asking how often we hear from him and what we write to him about. I wrote back but never heard back. Dee kept in touch for a little while but lost correspondence after that. She once told me how she received a letter from Richard saying that she was so saddened by his mail these days as each one could be the last, adding that he really didn't have long to go. By this, I took it that she meant until he was executed. Which I found odd, as anyone who was following his case knew that he wasn't going anywhere anytime soon. The appeals process meant that he would be sticking around for years, even decades.

I want to point out that at no time did I ever ask him about his crimes. For one, I knew all the details so there was no need. For two, I didn't feel comfortable asking; I didn't know how he'd react and I didn't want to risk our friendship. And for three, his outgoing mail was scrutinised and discussing his crimes almost certainly wouldn't have been permitted. Openly admitting to his crimes could have also jeopardised his appeals.

I told him about the horror action figures I collected; Pinhead, Jason, and Michael Myers. It was through him that I initially found out the original Michael Myers mask was a mould of William Shatner. Of course, he thought Pinhead kicked ass and pointed out there were no toys like that when he was free. Flying a kite was a big deal to him when he was a kid. I really couldn't believe this guy had done what he'd done. He was such a nice polite guy in his letters and possessed a real sense of humour. Every letter without fail he'd ask for 'Pics Of Chix.' He'd always thank me for the ones I'd sent in the previous letter saying they were excellent and to send more. This became a thorn in the side for my then jealous girlfriend who accused *me* of being a perv. I said 'Well that's what he wants, and if you're so bothered by me sending pictures of other women why don't you pose for some raunchy shots yourself?'

Now, I only meant this in an argumentative sense. But that's exactly what she opted for! I couldn't believe it! I'd get photos of her in lingerie, white satin panties and lacy bra with stockings and suspenders. I'd also get photos of her wearing sexy roleplay outfits I'd bought for her – French Maid and Naughty Nurse costumes. Of course, Rick loved this. He thought it was the greatest thing and couldn't get enough. He'd ask for more every letter. He told me how he had a picture of her on his cell wall. One we used for a club poster sitting in front of a pentagram wearing a PVC outfit and fishnet stockings holding a dagger.

Now you're probably wondering what kind of sicko sends provocative photos of his girlfriend in underwear to a serial killer? Well, put simply, I gave her the option of either sending random pictures of women from magazines and catalogues or sexy photos of her, and she opted for the latter without hesitation. Such were her insecurities that she would rather have the Night Stalker masturbating over her than me seeking out random pictures in magazines to send him!

He liked to ask a lot of random questions, like if I'd ever been skydiving, what my average days were like, if I liked exploring new places by myself or with someone else. Stuff that he couldn't do. Occasionally he'd comment on a photo from one of our club nights saying something of the effect of 'Looks like it was one hell of a party, I'd like to have been there!'

I often tried to imagine what Rick would be like in our world. Would I feel safe with him? If he was let loose upon society, would he return to his old ways? More so than ever, probably. You can't change who you really are. We might have struck up a friendship but, at the end of the day, he was still a killer.

2001 kicked off with the Big Day Out festival with *Limp Bizkit*, *PJ Harvey* and *Rammstein* headlining. Though I didn't do anything on the live music front until March that year, I toured Sydney industrial rock band *Scream Age* who had a look and sound similar to *White Zombie*. This coincided with the release of *The Exorcist – The Director's Cut*. It featured footage that was originally edited from the 1973 version including the possessed Regan spider walking down a staircase. Roadshow were handling the distribution and they provided me with movie passes, posters and a heap of flyers. The flyers were cool, they featured a couple of shots of Regan's possessed face and her levitating from the bed. I sent Rick a couple and he loved it. Said it was one of his favourite movies.

April saw UK black metal, goth band *Cradle Of Filth* touring their *Midian* album. I arranged an after-show party at the pub next door to the venue in Brisbane's Fortitude Valley. Our mates from Sydney, Psi-Kore, were supporting so they got us on the guest list and invited the band to the party afterwards. To my surprise, they all turned up. Frontman Dani Filth even announced it on stage! They brought their then female operatic vocalist, Sarah Jezebel Deva, on tour with them, and I didn't know this at the time but she also wrote to Richard Ramirez. It would have been interesting to swap stories. One of her letters from him features in Gavin Baddeley's historical biography of the band *The Gospel Of Filth*.

On June 11, 2001, Oklahoma Bomber Timothy McVeigh was executed by lethal injection for the 1995 bombing of a government building, which killed 168 people. He claimed he carried it out as revenge for the 1993 Waco siege of the Branch Davidian Cult's compound which left

86 people dead, many of whom were children. McVeigh, a gulf war veteran himself, saw this as an act of war by the United States Government on its own people. I asked Rick his thoughts on McVeigh and his response was that he was smart but hard to understand.

August saw *Slayer* back in town touring their new album *God Hates Us All*. It was a return to form for the band, as far as I was concerned from 1998's disappointing, *Diabolus In Musica*. The concert was at Brisbane's now defunct Festival Hall with *Machine Head* supporting. I arranged a huge after party with giveaway copies of the new album. Two bands I was managing – *Hollow* and *Post-Life Disorder* also played. Unlike *Cradle Of Filth*, none of *Slayer* turned up, though I wasn't expecting them to. Their profile was considerably higher than *Cradle*'s and they would have had a strict touring schedule to adhere to. It also would have been a nightmare for those guys has they would have been swamped.

The record company, who I did regular work with, provided me with a bunch of signed posters and after-party flyers though. I sent Rick one and he was really appreciative. He asked me if I'd ever met the guys from *Slayer*. I told him I had on their '98 tour at the Brisbane community radio station 4ZZZ fm.

In a sinister twist of fate, *Slayer*'s *God Hates Us All* was released in Australia before the U.S. It wasn't released in the States until that fateful day September 11, 2001 – the day that shook the world.

Of course, we talked about that. That's all you heard in the media 24/7 for weeks after. It was pretty hard to go *anywhere* without seeing Osama Bin Laden's image plastered over every single media outlet. He couldn't believe it when it happened either. Said it was just like a movie. I asked him his thoughts on George W. Bush and his administration, but he really wasn't into politics.

Sometimes I'd get impatient and send another letter whilst waiting for a reply from the previous one. This confused him somewhat. He thought maybe our letters were getting crossed.

Halloween 2001, I brought *Scream Age* back up from Sydney to perform. I had the place decked out in spooky decorations and candle lit Jack 'O Lanterns. Everyone turned up in costume. I had white ghoulish face paint with shades of black and grey in the form of a skull. He loved the photos and would have liked to have been there, adding that we looked ghoulish indeed.

The year ended with me touring Sydney electro, industrial band Jerk and putting on an after-party for U.S. band Fear Factory. Guitarist Dino Cazeres turned up and joined one of the bands on stage! I did the usual, sent photos and flyers etc.

2002 began with us moving into a new house. Then something happened, I wrote him several times but never heard back. I couldn't work out why, could have been anything, illness, punishment. I really didn't know what.

I wouldn't hear from him again for another three years.

The 1994 Electric Hellfire Club EP 'Satan's Little Helpers' featured Demonic caricatures of Richard Ramirez, Charles Manson, David Berkowitz and Aleister Crowley.

Richard Ramirez interview for Hustler magazine November 1993 Continues over pages.

RAMIREZ

"Satanists need to have more faith than Christians, because Christ was seen and felt. Lucifer has never felt the need to show himself, but in everyone's soul he can be felt."

"I want to say hello to the people of Los Angeles, and I miss them all. By the way, I think Los Angeles is a great city with its freeways."
—*Convicted Serial Killer Richard Ramirez*
June 2, 1993

* * *

In the summer of 1985, the people of Southern California were haunted by a string of Satanic-tinged slayings. It was as if Lucifer himself were cruising the L.A. freeways, joyriding from off-ramp to off-ramp, taking random exits and stealing into the residential night to burglarize, to thieve, to beat, strangle, rape, sodomize, shoot and slash throats in a savage rampage. News of gruesome assaults and murders spilled terror and dread from the southland's television screens. The roaming killer, while still at large, became known as the Night Stalker.

On August 30, 1985, an all-points bulletin was issued for Richard Ramirez, then 25, of Los Angeles. A photograph of the lanky, 6-1 Latino drifter from El Paso, Texas, was issued to the papers and TV. The fugitive was captured and stomped by an angry mob as he attempted to flee in a stolen car.

After a 16-month trial, during which the glowering defendant flashed satanic symbols and attracted a following of groupies, Ramirez was found guilty of 13 murders and 30 other felonies and sentenced to die.

Now housed in San Francisco's Hall of Justice county jail while awaiting trial on the murder of a man named Peter Pan, Ramirez met with HUSTLER for his first in-depth interview since being incarcerated.

* * *

RAMIREZ: Are you nervous? You have a lot of questions?
HUSTLER: Let's talk about girls first. Why are women so attracted to you?
RAMIREZ: Possibly because they can relate to me. The girls are nice to have in my situation, but I spend more time discussing the relationship than living it. But there are good friendships formed nevertheless.
HUSTLER: What was your success with women before?
RAMIREZ: Oh, I had no success at all. I would have women, but no long-term relationship. It was an on-and-off thing. After 1979 I was living on the fast lane in Southern California, and I didn't have time to romance, wine and dine.
HUSTLER: What kind of women are attracted to a convicted serial killer?
RAMIREZ: Someone who's probably interested in my situation and what I was accused of, the murders themselves. A lot of people are fascinated by death nowadays.
HUSTLER: Are these women looking for something?
RAMIREZ: A lot of them come into my life and leave. But I've known a lot of good people. A lot of good women. A lot of them are religious. They try to help me.
HUSTLER: Can you be helped by religion?
RAMIREZ: I'm pretty set in my ways. I doubt anything short of a miracle would change me, but I have an open mind, and listen to them.
HUSTLER: Were you brought up religious?
RAMIREZ: Very much so. My mother and my dad used to take me to church in Mexico and in my home state of Texas. They have huge cathedrals. I used to go into these places, and the ceilings were high up, and the aisles in the church gave me a sense that was very much bigger than life. Even though what I was seeing was porcelain, alabaster or whatever, right? Still, it took on a life of its own. These huge figures, the saints, the crucifixions. Religion played a big role in my life.
HUSTLER: It captured your imagination.
RAMIREZ: More than my imagination, I internalized it, and it became a part of every day life. How I thought. How I felt. Later on during my late teen years, it very much had conflict within me, because good and evil was in conflict within me, and still is—you know; bad and good and everything I had learned about Satan and God.
HUSTLER: Did you go around thinking that God was watching everything you did?
RAMIREZ: Yes. Actions in my life that I took, even then, I would always judge myself and try to fathom how God would judge me.
HUSTLER: How did you make out?
RAMIREZ: In my late teens it wasn't going too good. I got to be about 20 years old, and they really caused some problems within me.
HUSTLER: What were you doing?
RAMIREZ: Well, I started resorting to a life that...let's just say my mother wouldn't approve of. I had to fend for myself. I was thrown out in the world at an early age—17—and so it was a pretty hard life for me. I stole cars. I was a pickpocket. Stuff like that.
HUSTLER: What happened at home that you got thrown out?
RAMIREZ: I went to reform school for months when I was 17. When I came back I moved out. I sustained myself by selling drugs and stuff. And then I came to California.
HUSTLER: Do you believe Satan exists?
RAMIREZ: Yes, I believe he does. I believe evil is a force that is beyond us, and that I just have to invite him in, and he will.
HUSTLER: When did you actively bring Satan into your life?
RAMIREZ: It was about 1980, and I was hustling on the street, and I landed in jail

RAMIREZ

"The pictures that were shown at my trial were especially gruesome. Oh, they had shootings, stabbings, you know. People's heads almost severed."

a month or two—it was petty theft or something. I met up with this guy, and he was a Satan worshiper. For two months, I was with him. I came out of jail, but I never forgot what he said. And basically it was: Why worship the good guy, when you yourself are doing things that are not basically good? You would be on the fringes of society's rules. Somehow it just made sense to worship somebody who would protect you in whatever it is you were doing.

HUSTLER: What form did worship take?
RAMIREZ: It developed slowly. I started reading into the books, and then I started meeting certain people who were into the same thing—satanism. Satanists need to have more faith than Christians, because Christ was seen and felt. Lucifer has never felt the need to show himself, but in everyone's soul he can be felt. A lot of these clandestine cults practice satanism nowadays, but not in its violent form. They're only looking for a way to play at wickedness.
HUSTLER: Did you attend black masses?
RAMIREZ: Once only, but I kept my distance. I was not part of the group. It was at the cemetery, and it was at night. I really couldn't tell what they were doing. Me and a friend were at a distance, just watching them.
HUSTLER: So you were not a joiner?
RAMIREZ: I always kept my distance. I never trusted people. Even so, it was my undoing, even the little bit that I did trust them.
HUSTLER: How so?
RAMIREZ: People knew my lifestyle, and the connection was made by them—and eventually by the police—that because of my beliefs, I was the perfect candidate for being the Night Stalker.

*   *   *

Jennie Vincow, 79, stabbed to death. Dale Okazasi, 34, shot to death. Tsai-Lian Yu, 30, shot to death. Vincent Zazzara, 64, beaten to death, and his wife, Maxine Zazzara, stabbed to death. William Doi, 65, shot to death. Mabel Bell, 84, strangled. Mary Louise Cannon, 77, throat slashed. Joyce Lucille Nelson, 62, beaten to death. Maxon Kneiding, 68, and his wife, Lela, 66, both shot to death. Chainarong Khovananth, shot to death. Elyas Abowath, shot to death. One woman's eyes were gouged out in an "obscene" manner; one was raped and sodomized in front of her young son. Another was forced to swear allegiance to the devil. Superior Court Judge Michael Tynan characterized the crimes as displaying "cruelty, callousness and viciousness beyond any human understanding."

*   *   *

HUSTLER: What are some of the things you've been accused of?
RAMIREZ: I've been accused of almost every crime you can imagine.
HUSTLER: Can you describe the crime-scene photos that were shown at your trial?
RAMIREZ: Yes. When I was sitting at the defense table, they were passed around. They were shown to the jurors. In my opinion, it makes the jury biased by showing them these pictures in a criminal case. They showed pictures in color of people basically dead—and bloody. The pictures that were shown at my trial were especially gruesome. Oh, they had shootings, stabbings, you know. People's heads almost severed. I do remember them.
HUSTLER: At your trial, you went Hollywood with the dark shades and bad attitude. Were you enjoying the attention?
RAMIREZ: I can't say that it would have been better to stay in my cell, because the existence in jail is monotonous. But then again, going to trial was in itself very tiring for me. The glasses—they were prescription lenses, but I had them tinted. And I just don't like my photograph being taken as much as it was then. Did I enjoy it? Not particularly. I would have rather been in Hawaii on a beach.
HUSTLER: Your entire attitude seemed to be: "Fuck all you people."
RAMIREZ: I was receiving so much negative publicity, I wasn't going to give anyone the satisfaction of seeing me down. Besides that, I didn't feel down. And beyond that, the image I projected was beyond me. The media portrayed this image of me as being a monster, ruthless, cold-hearted. But I'm not really that way. I'm more down to earth. So I let people think whatever they wanted to think. You see the crimes, and you can only imagine what kind of individual would do those crimes.
HUSTLER: The crimes were committed with "cruelty, callousness and viciousness beyond any human understanding."
RAMIREZ: It is not beyond understanding. Mankind has been like that throughout his history. Then again, in today's society people use those qualities—I call them qualities—for all things. It is for self-gratification. It is for sex. It is to quench hate and anger. For money. For excitement. A combination of all these, by whatever name, self-interest, anger, greed. They are very dangerous. This kind of fervor serves its own purpose. It doesn't obey rules. It runs amok. You see it on the news every day. But society cannot hang its moral and ethical values on me to survive. I do what I must in all ways, and I'm proud of it. The necessity to be myself supercedes all moral constraints.

(continued on page 104)

RAMIREZ (continued from page 64)

"I saw my cousin shoot his wife. His wife was dead. And the bed was bloody. It was where she had landed by the bullet. She got a .38 in the face."

HUSTLER: Have you been reading a lot?
RAMIREZ: Yes. I read. I suggest this book to everybody. It's called *Mysterious Stranger* by Mark Twain, and it's about Satan and his visit here. That's a good book. I read suspense and horror. Something that intrigues me. I have always been fascinated by death.
HUSTLER: Is death sexual?
RAMIREZ: Death sexual? It can be. Next to self-preservation, the sex drive is the most powerful human motivator. That's a good one for your magazine!
HUSTLER: When did you first start thinking about death?
RAMIREZ: When I was 11, I had an episode in my life. I saw my cousin shoot his wife, and that was very—I wouldn't say traumatic, but the shock value.... And especially when I went to the apartment later on with my dad to pick up some things that my cousin wanted to be picked up because he was in jail at the time already, and his wife was dead. And the bed was bloody. It was where she had landed by the bullet. She got a .38 in the face. And at the time it was very.... The stillness of the room, the eeriness, the must, you know. We had to open up the windows to ventilate the room. And it was something. I felt something. It was...it was...it was death! Because I had known the woman! I had known her very well. And then I went into the living room, and I saw her purse, and I looked through her purse, and I saw her identification, and I saw her things. It was a very strange feeling. That was the first time I ran across death. Ever since then, I was intrigued by it.
HUSTLER: What is blood to you?
RAMIREZ: Blood is the very substance that enables any living thing to exist. But blood is blood. I have heard of people drinking each other's blood. They cut each other, and they drink it, and it's supposed to be a euphoric feeling. So, you know, blood has no special interest for me. Blood is blood.
HUSTLER: Do you believe that when someone kills somebody, they take that person's power?
RAMIREZ: That belief has been known to exist for a long, long time. Dating back to the Inca and Maya periods in Mexico. Very long time ago. Sacrifices that were made on top of the altars and the pyramids included cannibalism of the heart and stuff. It is a possibility.

Me, myself, I've had no experience with it.

* * *

Richard Ramirez's remarks to the court before being sentenced to death: "It's nothing for you to understand, but I do have something to say. I have a lot to say, but now is not the time or the place. I don't know even why I'm wasting my breath, but what the hell.

"For so what is said of my life, there have been lies in the past, and there will be lies in the future. I don't believe in the hypocritical, moralistic dogma of this so-called civilized society. I need not look beyond this room to see all the liars, the haters, the killers, the crooks, the paranoid cowards. Truly the trematodes [parasitic flatworms] of the earth, each one of his own legal profession.

"You maggots, hypocrites one and all. We are all expendable for a cause. No one knows that better than those who kill for policy, clandestinely or openly as to the governments of the world, which kill in the name of God and country and for whatever else they deem appropriate. I don't need to hear all of society's rationalizations. I've heard them before, and the fact remains that what is, is. You don't understand me. You are not expected to. You are not capable of it.

"I am beyond your experience. I am beyond good and evil. Legions of the night, nightbreed. Repeat not the errors of night prowler, and show no mercy. I will be avenged. Lucifer dwells in us all. That's it."

* * *

HUSTLER: In your statement, you said, "Repeat not the errors of night prowler." What were night prowler's errors?
RAMIREZ: I could lie to you, man, and say a bunch of things, but at the time I was under a lot of stress. If my memory serves me correctly, I just meant not to believe in the system. Don't for a minute think you'll get a fair shake in these circumstances and, above all, nobody should want to be in here. And I advise...how should I put this? Let me just say, read a lot and find out what the world is about and especially what you yourself are about. It's easy to be deceived and to deceive yourself. But ask yourself questions. Who you are. That was my mistake during the years of my life.
HUSTLER: What were the errors?
RAMIREZ: Be aware of your actions before you find yourself in a vicious predicament.
HUSTLER: Who are "the legions of the night"?
RAMIREZ: The legions of the night are the people who exult in the hour of darkness in which the power of evil is exalted. These are the people who know of the moral sense, the moral sense being the faculty that enables mankind to distinguish between right and wrong. Nevertheless, an evildoer believes that what he does is right just as much as a good person knows that his actions are right. And so who is to

RAMIREZ

"I believe that the bulk of humanity is equivalent to a herd of cattle. Everyone plays a role, and no one really says what is truly on their mind."

question who? Because of society's laws and man's rules and God's rules. The people know who I am talking about. They are the ones who have felt that they are not of the majority. They have different feelings and attitudes. But I believe that the bulk of humanity is equivalent to a herd of cattle. Everyone plays a role, and no one really says what is truly on their mind.

HUSTLER: When you were sentenced to the gas chamber, you said, "Big deal. Death always went with the territory." What territory?

RAMIREZ: That was my life. I lived a dangerous life. Whether I was riding in a stolen car, which I was...at any point in time I could have been killed or died; so nothing in existence holds any terror for me. Certainly when I was sentenced to death, it didn't hold anything for me.

HUSTLER: What about now?

RAMIREZ: Even less so. I don't have any fear of death. Death comes to all of us eventually. Every day inside this place is a day I'll never get back. One wasted day after another adds up to wasted years. So whatever comes my way, I'm pretty willing to accept. All I can do is put up a fight, and beyond that it's out of my hands, and that's it. You understand, I don't think there's much hope for me. But still, I never know what's in the cards.

HUSTLER: When did you lose your fear?

RAMIREZ: If something is done enough, you become immune to it. You become immune to the feeling, but the adrenaline and the rush of excitement is never gone.

HUSTLER: Does the Night Stalker deserve the gas chamber?

RAMIREZ: The district attorneys have as much scorn and hatred and they muster it toward a defendant that is being held for murder, and the want for his blood is felt. But the district attorney puts it under the banner of justice. It's a blood lust, if you ask me. And when the state comes to execute a man, they laugh. How many burly guards come calling? Do you know what I'm saying? The state risks nothing! A judge and district attorneys throughout the state, throughout the country, have the power to commit murder with impunity.

HUSTLER: What's your reaction to all the hate directed toward you?

RAMIREZ: When I first got arrested, a lot of things bothered me. But then again, they didn't, because once you've heard some things, you've heard it all; so you become immune to the negativity. If indeed I did do these crimes, then the relatives of the victims are entitled to their hate. What puzzles me is how people can care about strangers. That doesn't click in me. Why should I care if John Doe down the street gets run over by a car? I don't. But a lot of people do because it's part of humanity; they have feelings and whatever toward strangers, and I don't. I don't care a fuck what happens to anybody I don't know. And I don't put my business in other people's business, which a lot of people tend to do. I felt animosity from those around me and from what I read, but I don't waste my energy or anger on people or even the television.

HUSTLER: Are you still beyond good and evil?

RAMIREZ: Everybody has good and evil in them, and so even though I'd like to be 100-percent evil, I'm not.

HUSTLER: What's something good about you that you wish you could change?

RAMIREZ: I'm too easy-going sometimes. Then again, anger and hate, while some people can cope with it, I cannot. I cannot maintain my anger and hate to a level that I can live comfortably with it. It causes me headaches and stuff. When I get angry, it is an extreme form. It's the extreme. There's no in-between. So I have to try and calm myself. I've meditated over the years, and I exercise.

HUSTLER: Is this since you were convicted?

RAMIREZ: The first year I was very much a problem for the sheriff's department. But I said to myself, "I gotta go through this. I gotta do this, and I need to calm down." I looked into relaxation techniques, meditation techniques, so that I could go through this phase in my life without constantly having my mind in upheaval.

HUSTLER: What's your favorite section of HUSTLER Magazine?

RAMIREZ: The parody section [*Bits & Pieces*]. After all, life is a joke, and I enjoy when you make light of something that other people take so fucking seriously. In the long run, we all die, and nothing really matters, like Freddie Mercury says. And I understand you can't be on my side. Don't try to favor me 'cause you'll get a bunch of those letters.

HUSTLER: We'll get a bunch of those letters no matter what we do.

RAMIREZ: Listen! People are intrigued. I'm telling you. People, they don't really know what the fuck they want. It's like, they say no, but they mean yes.

HUSTLER: How will you be avenged?

RAMIREZ: I'm an angry motherfucker. And I just hope all those who are deserving get what they got coming. I'll leave it at that.

HUSTLER: Are you confident that people get what they have coming?

RAMIREZ: Pieces of shit are killed every day.

* * *

"Keep the evil thought."

—*Richard Ramirez*
June 3, 1993

American shock rock band, *Marilyn Manson*, members combined the first names of female sex symbols and the last names of infamous serial killers as a juxtaposition of American pop culture icons - Gidget Gein, Daisy Berkowitz, Madonna Wayne Gacy, and Twiggy Ramirez were just some of the members in previous line ups.

Early Marilyn Manson flyer depicting Night Stalker Richard Ramirez

Every letter Richard would request 'Pics of Chix.' So, I would send him racy photos of women in lingerie, bikinis and sexy roleplay costumes – French Maid and Naughty Nurse.

Some of Richard's letters.

'Toolbox Killer' Lawrence Bittaker was a Death Row neighbour in San Quentin

Nico Claux – The Vampire of Paris was also a penpal of Richard's. Rick sent me some of his artwork which unfortunately I no longer have.

Rick's drawing of Marvel supervillain Venom.

Chapter Four

Back In Touch

So, was Richard Ramirez evil incarnate? There are those out there that would certainly believe he was. Particularly families of the victims. He has always argued however that mankind has been bloodthirsty throughout history, and that we are a predatory species by nature. Adding that serial killers do what governments do on a grand scale, killing is killing whether it's done for duty, profit or pleasure. So therefore, society had no business hanging its moral ethical values on him.

There is indeed some truth to this argument. Particularly, when you look at the wholesale global slaughter throughout the ages. The atomic holocaust on Hiroshima and Nagasaki, the bombing of Dresden, Auschwitz and the deluge of napalm that rained on Vietnam. All justified as 'casualties of war.'

Something certainly moulded Richard, but it wasn't the Prince of Darkness's doing; nor was heavy metal to blame. In reality it had more to do with a psychopathic Vietnam veteran cousin who murdered his wife in front of him and taught young Richard 'the ropes.' Add to that, violent, sexual fantasies fuelled by chronic substance abuse to the point of being unable to distinguish between fantasy and reality, and you have the volatile ingredients for a violent sociopath.

Unfortunately, I no longer have any of the letters in my possession from my initial correspondence with him. I went through a nasty, messy break up with the ex and anyone who has gone through something similar will understand what I'm talking about. She figured that since they were also addressed to her and she posed for photographs, she was entitled to them. But that's another story. What you see in the following pages is all I have. His 'doctor's handwriting' is extremely hard to read, so I've retyped some of them and provided explanations for some of the content.

I was browsing the true crime section of a bookstore one day when I spotted an updated paperback version of Philip Carlo's *The Night Stalker*. It featured a new extra chapter on his Death Row marriage to Doreen Lioy. This prompted me to resume my correspondence with him. And whilst we're on the subject of Carlo's book, as much as I enjoy and recommend it, there's something I want to amend, which I believe to be pure fabrication.

Zeena Lavey visited Richard in jail whilst awaiting trial. It states that Zeena told Richard that her father and the Church of Satan were praying to Satan for him and were going to make him an honorary member.

Anton Lavey would NOT do this. The Church of Satan does not condone murder; only in a self-defence life threatening situation. It also fiercely advocates taking responsibility for one's own actions. So, if you do commit murder be prepared for the consequences. No Satan is going to save you, that is reality.

Gothic singer, Eva O, formerly of Christian Death spent a lot of time with him, even claiming to be in a relationship with him, expressing the desire to have sex with him in her coffin that she slept in every night. I'm not refuting this; Eva O is renowned for having battled personal demons throughout the years. She later converted to Christianity and went by the name Eva O Halo. But later renounced her faith.

In Blanche Barton's authorised biography of Anton Lavey, *The Secret Life Of A Satanist*, Lavey claims to have met Richard Ramirez on the street. He stopped him in the street and said, 'Excuse me Mr. Lavey, could I talk to you for a few minutes?' Lavey told him he didn't do business on the street, but he could write to the P.O. Box. Richard apologized for bothering him saying he just wanted to ask him a couple of questions and wished him a happy Solstice. Lavey regretted giving the young Richard the brush off, as he seemed like such a nice polite young kid.

I photocopied the segment of that page and sent it to Rick asking him about this incident. He replied that he didn't recall meeting Anton on the street and joked that he was probably too drunk to remember.

So, I wrote him, told him it's been a while and I was now single and living in a new place. It didn't take long for a reply and we resumed contact. He said he'd tried writing me but never heard back, which I found strange, as I'd sent him multiple letters since we last corresponded but never mind. Of course, one of the first sentences was 'Send Pics of Chix.' Of course, I was happy to do this but San Quentin had cracked down on what inmates could receive and all nudity was now banned. He told me to cover all nude spots with a felt pen or draw a bikini on them. I did this and they were still sent back to me. The trouble is, it wasn't just the pictures they sent back, it was the whole package including the letter, which was a huge fucking hassle. I got several packages returned and told him that I just couldn't risk it anymore. He'd just have to settle for no nude pics – bikini and lingerie clad chicks.

He told me he would be happy with that and also offered to put me in touch with chicks that wrote to him from Australia since I was now single. He offered to give out my email address and phone number which actually produced results! I'll get to that later. I told him I was still promoting bands and movies and sent him promo flyers and photos along with the 'Pics of Chix.'

How'd ya like that? The Night Stalker Dating Service!

MARCEESE,

GREETINGS. RECIEVED YOUR LETTER ALONG WITH THE PIC OF DEVILLA. DO YOU HAVE ANY OF HER ON HOOKAH OR OTHER PAGAN? HOW LONG WERE YOU WITH HER? DON'T HAVE ACCESS TO ANY PICS OF ME AT THE MOMENT. SOON AS I DO I'LL SEND ONE ALONG. HAVEN'T HEARD OF THAT SITE YOU MENTION ON EBAY. YOU HAVE AN EMAIL ADDRESS? YOU KNOW A GUY NAMED ANDREW? HE WORKS WITH BANDS IN YOUR COUNTRY. RECENTLY SAW GHOST RIDER. IT WAS OK. SEEN ANY GOOD MOVIES? WHATS YOUR AVERAGE DAY LIKE? THATS ALL FOR NOW. TAKE CARE

YOUR FRIEND
RICHARD

MARCEESE
THE SENTINEL
2 LINUM PLACE

Gothic singer, Eva O, spent a lot of time with Richard Ramirez when he was first apprehended. Even claiming to be in a relationship with him. She was married to former Christian Death frontman, Rozz Williams, who hung himself on April 1, 1998. She later married Kettle Cadaver frontman, Edwin Borsheim, who committed suicide on June 20, 2017.

Eva on stage with Shadow Project 1992

MARCEESE,

RECIEVED A COUPLE OF YOUR LETTERS ALONG WITH PAGES OF CHIX. THANKS. THEY WERE EXCELLENT. THINK YOU COULD SEND SOME ON KODAK PICTURE PAPER AND COVER ANY NUDE SPOTS WITH CRAYON OR DRY ERASER PEN. SO WHEN ITS SUMMER OVER HERE ITS WINTER THERE? ENCLOSED IS A SIGNED PHOTO. RECENTLY SAW TRISTAN AND ISOLDE. IT WAS OK. IT WAS ABOUT THE BRITISH FIGHTING THE IRISH BACK IN THE ~~MEDIEVAL~~ MEDIEVAL DAYS. I BELIEVE BIANCHI IS IN WALLA WALLA IN WASHINGTON. NO I DIDNT HEAR ABOUT THAT EVENT IN LA. WHAT WAS IT ABOUT? SO WHAT ARE YOUR AVERAGE DAYS LIKE? SO HOWS IT GOING WITH LYDIA? EVER SEEN A MOVIE WHERE THE MAIN CHARACTERS NAME IS QUIGLEY. ITS FILMED IN AUSTRALIA AND IT TAKES PLACE BACK IN THE FRONTIER DAYS. ITS PRETTY INTERESTING. I SEE THAT AUSTRALIA HAS

SOME ... VAST OPEN PLAINS. ANYWAY
THATS ALL FOR NOW WRITE WHEN
YOU GET A CHANCE.
                    YOUR FRIEND
                       RICHARD

MARCEESE
~~~~~~~~~~
19 MONTANUS DR
BELLBOWRIE Q 4070
AUSTRALIA

He's referring to Kenneth Bianchi – one of the Hillside Stranglers, the L.A. event was 6/6/06 organised by the Church of Satan. Lydia is a chick I was seeing.

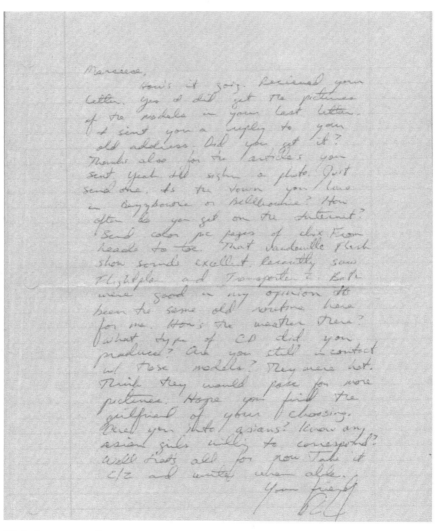

This letter reads –

Marceese,

How's it going. Received your letter, yes I did get the pictures of the models in your last letter. I sent you a reply to your old address. Did you get it? Thanks also for the articles you sent. Yeah I'll sign a photo, just send one. Is the town you live in Bezzbowrie or Bellbowrie? How often do you get on the internet? Send color pic pages of chix from head to toe. That Feasting the Flesh show sounds excellent - (It was a stage production with erotic and cannibalistic themes playing in Brisbane at the time). Recently saw *Flightplan* and *Transporter 2*. Both were good in my opinion. It's been the same old routine here for me. How's the weather there? What type of CD did you produce? – (my band at the time had just recorded an E.P.). Are you still in contact with those models? They were hot – (I'd hired models dressed as characters from my comic book I produced for the Sexpo exhibition in Brisbane). Think they would pose for more pictures? Hope you find the girlfriend of your choosing. Are you into Asians? Know any Asian girls willing to correspond? Well that's all for now. Take it E/Z and write when able'

Your Friend
Rick

MMCEBE,

"GREETINGS. HOWS EVERYTHING GOING? I SENT A FEW CHIX YOUR NUMBER. TAKE SOME PICS OF EM SHOULD YOU DECIDE TO MEET EM. RECENTLY SAW FANTASTIC 4 AND NEXT GOOD MOVIES. HAVE YOU BEEN TO THE BEACH? I KNOW ITS SUMMERTIME THERE. DO ANYTHING SPECIAL FOR NEW YEARS EVE? I KNOW AUSTRALIA PUTS ON A BIG FIREWORKS DISPLAY. IS YOUR BAND STILL PLAYING? THATS ALL FOR NOW TAKE IT EZ WRITE WHEN ABLE.

YOUR FRIEND
RICHARD

MARLEESE,

THANKS FOR THE CLAUX ARTICLE. IT WAS INTERESTING. AND FOR THE PIC/AGES OF THE GIRLS. I ALSO GOT THE NOTE FROM MORBID DOES HE GO BY THE NAME OF OZ? AND ALSO RECIEVED THE ETCHING OF BON SCOTTS PLACE. YES THEY SHOW HORROR MOVIES HERE BUT NOTHING GRAPHIC. NOTHING LIKE HOSTEL OR SAW. I'VE HEARD ZODIAC WAS GOOD. READ THE BOOK MANY YEARS AGO. HOW DID THE EVENT YOU HAVE ON JUNE 23 GO? YOU HAVE AN EMAIL ADDRESS CORRECT? DO YOU HAVE PICS POSTED UP ON THE SITE? WHEN DOES YOUR MUSIC FESTIVAL TAKE PLACE? YEAH I WRITE TO A FEW AUSTRALIAN GIRLS. I'LL SEND EM YOUR #. IN FACT IF YOU HEAR FROM A GIRL NAMED LINDA IN THE U.K. THAT WILL BE MY FRIEND THERE. I'M NOT INTO POLITICS. NO I'VE NOT SEEN ANY OSBOURNE EPISODES. THATS ON CABLE. ONLY BASIC TV CHANNELS HERE. YES I DID KNOW ABOUT THE SONG HOTEL CALIFORNIA. ITS A GOOD SONG.

San Francisco is a good tourist spot. Alcatraz is a place to visit. I used to hang around Fishermans Wharf. Lots of shops and places to see. Let Oz know I can't recieve CD's here. Thanks for the offer though. I'll end here. Take care and write when you get a chance.

     Your Friend
     Richard

Marleese
The Sentinel
2 Linum Pl
Bellbowrie
QLD 4070
Australia

Whilst in Perth, my housemate, Desset, visited Bon Scott's grave and got an etching, which I sent him. The June 23rd date was a Winter Solstice celebration. I asked him about George W. Bush that's why he responded that he wasn't into politics.

Bon Scott's grave. My housemate at the time got an etching which I sent him. I did ask him about the Metallica concert they played at San Quentin on May 1, 2003. He responded that he was in a lock down unit therefore couldn't attend. I guess Death Row would be.

Marceese,

How's it going? Hope good. Thanks for the pic pages of the girls. Send more. Did a girl named Sarah contact you? I didn't recognize the name Keza. I don't have access to the internet no. Saw the movie 'War Rogue'. It was ok. Not much new happening here. What's the fastest you've gone in a car? How do you get around the city? That's all for now. Take it EZ. Write when you get a chance. Glad to hear your band is doing good.

Your friend
RL

This letter reads –

Marceese,

How's it going? Received your package, you should send pic pages of girls in separate envelopes from your letters. Just include a short note, Haven't seen any of the *Saw* movies. Hope you have a good New Year's Eve. Passed along your # to that girl in Australia, her name is Anna. I've seen a poster for the movie *The Descent*, good drawing. Did you have a good birthday? Did you get those tattoos? You know a chick named Sarah Jane? She was in a heavy metal band that toured Europe and the UK. Can't recall the name of the band though – (this was Sarah Jezebel Deva from *Cradle Of Filth*). I and her correspond now and then. Yes I've read books by Lovecraft, good stuff. That's all for now. Take it E/Z and have a drink on me.

Your Friend
Rick

Yes, Anna did get in touch with me. She initially sent a text message which was soon followed by lengthy phone calls. She was an attractive blonde girl from Sydney originally from Poland. It was kind of surreal, the Night Stalker had set me up with someone! I mean how many people can seriously say they met through an infamous serial killer! People kind of freaked out when I told them. Anna came to Brisbane to visit me. We spent the night together in a hotel drinking, nothing came of it though. We were just too different, she was a straight girl, Polish and a devout Catholic. And here's me, a black clad member of the Church of Satan! We did keep in touch for a while but lost contact after that. I'll give Rick this though he was looking out for me!

Marcese,

Greetings. Recieved your letter. Have you read Revolver magazine? It has some good heavy metal articles in it. I do remember seeing The Warriors. Good movie. Comic books are ok. The pages you sent were cool. I did have a hearing on the date you mention but was unable to attend. I used to write Nico Claux years ago. He's a good artist. Saw the movie "Into the Wild". Its a true story about a guy who hitch hikes to Alaska w/out telling his parents. Send more pictures of girls. Whats been the best and first concert you attended? Mine was Black Sabbath. Whats been the best year you've had? My worst was when I got arrested. If you could experience anything what would it be? I always wanted to try skydiving but never got around to it. I read its expensive. Write when you get a chance.

Richard

MARCEESE,

How it going? Thanks for the material you sent. The pix of the chix were great. Send more. Include a nude page or two just cover any nude spots with a red crayon. Draw a bikini. Yeah I enjoyed Alien vs Predator. I don't have any pictures of myself at the moment. Soon as I get one I'll send it along. No not allowed nude photos here anymore. When you send photos of chix try and make them from head to toe. Barefoot if possible. I did read a book about the Zodiac a long time ago. It was pretty good. You mention the movie Dirty Harry, have you seen Magnum Force? What concerts have you been to? Do you have a CD player or do you prefer iPod? Saw The Cave not too long ago. It was ok. Kinda dark though. Take it e/z. Your friend
RICHARD

July/2010

Marceese

Greetings. Thanks for the pictures. Send more. I'll see if I can find you any girls. Yes I do remember the magazine "Answer Me". It was good. I used to read it years ago. Who wrote the book? If you send nude pics of girls just cover nude spots by drawing bikini w/ expo pen. I've included some pics for you. Would you ever sail long distance in a small sailing craft? Have you ever gone skiing? Do you watch a movie a 2nd or 3rd time or only once? Do you like making new friends? When you visit a strange city do you like to explore it by yourself or w/ someone? That's all for now. Take care, write when you get a chance.

Young friend

DRAWING ENCLOSED

This letter reads –

Marceese,

Greetings, thanks for the pictures, send more. I'll see if I can find you any girl . Yes, I do remember the magazine 'Answer Me!,' it was good, I read it years ago. Who wrote the book? If you send nude pics of girls just cover nude spots by drawing bikini with felt pen. I've included some jokes for you. Would you ever sail long distance in a sailing craft? Have you ever gone skiing? Do you watch a movie 2 or 3 times or only once? Do you like making new friends? When you visit a strange city do you like to explore it yourself or with someone? That's all for now. Take care to write when you get a chance.
Your Friend
Rick

DRAWING ENCLOSED

Must have been a fan of Spidey villains. Previous drawing was Venom!

> MARLEESE,
> GREETINGS. THANKS FOR THE PIC PAGES OF THE GIRLS IN YOUR AUG 15 LETTER. SOUNDS LIKE YOU SAW SOME GOOD MOVIES, CAN'T SAY I REMEMBER 'THE CAR'. WHO DIRECTED AND STARRED IN IT? HOPE YOU HAVE A GOOD BIRTHDAY. HAVE A DRINK ON ME. CAN'T SAY I REMEMBER MEETING ANTON. I MIGHT OF — JUST TOO DRUNK TO REMEMBER HER. YOU WRITE ANNA IS IN THE UK. WHO'S ANNA? OH — THE CHICK I INTRODUCED YOU TO. COOL. TELL HER I SAID HI. STILL TRYING TO FIND YOU ANOTHER ONE. HAVENT HEARD OF THE GERMAN GUY WHO POSTED AN AD — NO. SOUNDS STRANGE. THATS ALL FOR NOW. E/Z
> RICHARD

I asked him about German cannibal Armin Meiwes who posted an ad on the internet for a voluntary victim to be eaten and got one.

MARLEESE,

HOWS IT GOING? RECIEVED YOUR LETTER. RESEND THE PICTURE PAGES OF THE GIRLS BUT WITH NO RETURN ADDRESS. I DON'T KNOW WHY THEY WERE RETURNED TO YOU. SEND SOME IN LINGERIE OR BIKINI. DID YOU COVER NUDE SPOTS WITH A CRAYON? SOMETIME PICTURES ARE BETTER THAN PAGES. I GAVE YOUR NAME AND ADDRESS TO A GIRL NAMED ANNA. SHE LIVES IN AUSTRALIA AS WELL. LET ME KNOW IF SHE CONTACTS YOU. DID YOU GO TO ANY OF THE CONCERT SHOWS YOU MENTION? SEND 40 ENVELOPES AND 50 SHEETS OF WRITING PAPER IF POSSIBLE. HOW DO YOU SPELL THE NAME OF THE STREET YOU LIVE IN?

I DON'T HAVE A PICTURE OF MYSELF AT THE MOMENT BUT IF YOU CAN GET ONE SEND IT AND I'LL SIGN IT FOR YOU. READ ANY BOOKS LATELY? HAVE YOU BEEN TO THE BEACH? IF SO TAKE SOME PICS OF THE GIRLS FOR ME. SO DO YOU GET HUSTLER ON A REGULAR BASIS? RECENTLY SAW ULTRAVIOLET. ITS A SCI FI THRILLER ABOUT A CHICK WHO SAVES A KID NAMED SIX. ANYWAY THATS ALL FOR NOW. TAKE IT E/Z. WRITE WHEN ABLE. YOUR FRIEND
　　　　　　　　　　　　RICHARD

Marceese,

Greetings. I'll have to pass on answering most of your questions. Hope thats ok with you. Yes I saw the original Hitcher a long time ago. It was good. Recently saw Fearless w/ Jet Li. It was good also good. Yes you can try sending me a copy of your publication. Not sure if I'll get it though. I am familiar w/ thrash metal yes but it gets no radio play around here. I did meet Zeena. She was cool. I wonder what shes doing these days. What else have you been up to? Thats all for now. Thanks for sending the seperate package. Havent recieved it yet but will look for it.   Your friend
                                        Richard

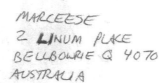

MARCEESE
2 LINUM PLACE
BELLBOWRIE Q 4070
AUSTRALIA

MARCEESE,

HOWS IT GOING? RECIEVED YOUR MARCH 20 LETTER. ENCLOSED IS THE SIGNED PHOTO. NO I DIDNT GET THE CALENDAR YOU SENT. AT LEAST NOT YET. DID YOU GO SEE 300? HAVE YOU BOUGHT A COMPUTER? HOW DID THE CONCERT GO? RECENTLY SAW CASINO ROYALE AND FLY BOYS. GOOD MOVIES. HOW FAR IS THE BEACH FROM WHERE YOU LIVE? I HEARD PAUL STANLEY OF KISS DID A CONCERT IN YOUR COUNTRY RECENTLY. ALSO READ THAT DIO IS PLAYING W/ SABBATH ON THEIR MOST RECENT TOUR. THATS ALL FOR NOW. TAKE IT E/Z WRITE WHEN YOU GET A CHANCE.

YOUR FRIEND
RICHARD

MARLEESE

    GREETINGS. THANKS FOR THE PICS. SAY HI TO MERLE FOR ME. I DID HEAR OF THE BAD WEATHER YOUR HAVING. HOPE ITS CLEARED UP BY NOW. VERONICA LOOKS GOOD. DO YOU HAVE A FAVORITE AUTHOR — BOOK? SEND PAGES FROM COMIC BOOKS. ONES I CAN DRAW FROM. WHICH IS YOUR FAVORITE DRINK? I USED TO LIKE JACK DANIELS. WHAT TYPE OF CAMERA DO YOU HAVE? SEEN ANY GOOD MOVIE. WRITE WHEN YOU GET A CHANCE. YOUR FRIEND

               RICHARD

QUESTIONS — JOKES
DRAWING ENCLOSED

And this was the last I heard from him. I did write him and let him know that I would be in San Francisco in the coming weeks and requested he send visit forms but to no avail. Apparently, he ceased seeing any visitors in his final couple of years. Maybe his illness had really kicked in by then and he just didn't want anyone seeing him incapacitated? I really wish I had visited him though. San Quentin's visiting days are Saturday and Sunday, so I would have had to work it around my travel schedule.

Merle, he's referring to is Merle Allin – GG's brother. I'd spoken to Merle a while back on the phone. His number was in the back of the book I'd purchased 'I Was a Murder Junkie,' by Evan Cohen. It documents the last tour and days of GG Allin. I just called him up out of the blue and we had a lengthy conversation! We spoke of our mutual correspondence with Richard and other serial killers Merle wrote to, about when I saw his band The Murder Junkies when they toured Australia in 2010. I got Merle to sign the book along with other stuff and I sent Rick a photo of myself and Merle.

The bad weather he's referring to is the 2011 Brisbane floods. Where I am, we were cut off and without power for a week. Half the suburb was underwater. Veronica was a Ukrainian girl I met on an online dating site. She was based in Crimea and I was heading to see her on the same trip. I sent him a couple of her photos just to show him who I was now dating.

The last package I sent him was in February 2013 for his

birthday. He passed away in June that year. He did include some jokes and questions in his last letter which he wanted me to make multiple copies of and send back. No doubt to send out to his other penpals.

I've included them on the following pages.

JOKES — A GUY GETS HIS HAND STUCK INSIDE A VENDING MACHINE WHEN THEY ARE TRYING TO FREE HIM THEY ASK IF HE'S HOLDING ON TO SOMETHING YES HE SAYS THE SODA CAN — A SMALL BOY WAKES UP SEVERAL NIGHTS IN A ROW WHEN HE HEARS THUMPING SOUNDS COMING FROM HIS PARENTS BEDROOM HE ASKS HIS MOM ONE MORNING HOW COME SHE WAS JUMPING ON HIS DAD TO MAKE HIM LOSE WEIGHT SHE SAYS WELL THAT WONT WORK CAUSE THE LADY NEXT DOOR COMES OVER AND BLOWS HIM UP AGAIN

Could you make ten copies

QUESTIONS...

Who do you find yourself hanging out with more girlfriends or guyfriends? If you could be in any movie which one would it be? What was your first girlfriend like?

Below – Zeena and Nikolas Schreck attended Richard's trial.

Me and Merle Allin

The Murder Junkies 2010 Australian tour poster. Drummer Dino is wearing a Richard Ramirez shirt.

I sent him photos of Veronica, a Ukrainian girl I was dating at the time.

Serial killer chic and collectibles; trading card, patch and 'sign of horns' shirt.

Chad Morbid's daughter, Samael, displays iconic pentagram hand shirt.

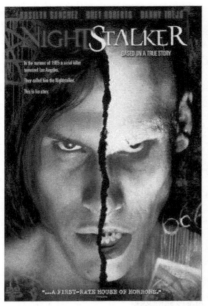

There have been three movies based on the Night Stalker case. The first was a 1989 made for TV movie mentioned at the start of this book, titled *Manhunt: Search For The Night Stalker*. Being a TV movie, it is a moderate but accurate account of what took place. *Nightstalker* (2002), on the other hand, is completely embellished with irrelevant sequences. Almost to the point that it totally detracts from the actual story. It was directed by Chris Fisher and stars Bret Roberts in the leading role. It depicts Richard Ramirez driving around, hunting his prey listening to guttural growling death metal. He was a big AC/DC fan and death metal wasn't even around then. It's also made up of multiple sequences of frenetic editing and demonic visions. I guess this is the movie's attempt to put you in the mindset of a crack smoking serial killer who believes to be possessed. It's also made up of fictional characters so if you're someone who takes an interest in the case, I advise you not to watch this movie. *The Night Stalker* (2016) was directed by Megan Griffiths and

stars Lou Diamond Phillips in the leading role and Bellamy Young. It tells the story of Kit, a female lawyer who's representing a drifter about to be executed. The only hope for her client is to visit Richard Ramirez on death row and get him to confess to the crime her client has been found guilty of. Of course, Ramirez, at first, is uncooperative but throughout the movie they almost develop a 'Clarice Starling/Hannibal Lecter' relationship. Phillips is a good role choice for Ramirez but the storyline isn't fact based. He was also portrayed by Anthony Ruivivar in the *American Horror Story* episode 'Devil's Night' from the fifth season 'Hotel.' It's an annual gathering featuring fellow serial killers, Jeffrey Dahmer, Aileen Wuornos, John Wayne Gacy and the Zodiac Killer. Both the *Electric Hellfire Club* and serial killer themed band, *Macabre*, have written songs about him; 'Jack the Knife' from the *EHC* album 'Kiss the Goat' (1995), and 'Night Stalker' from the *Macabre* album 'Sinister Slaughter' (1993) respectively.

He also appeared on the front cover of Swedish extreme metal band The Haunted's 2000 album 'Made Me Do It' along with the likes of Jeffrey Dahmer, Albert Fish, Tex Watson, Columbine High School killers Eric Harris and the Unabomber. The concept being that metal all too often is used as a scapegoat.

Anthony Ruivivar as Richard Ramirez in *American Horror Story*.

The Electric Hellfire Club's 1995 *Kiss The Goat* album features the song 'Jack the Knife.' And below Macabre's 1993 album *Sinister Slaughter*.

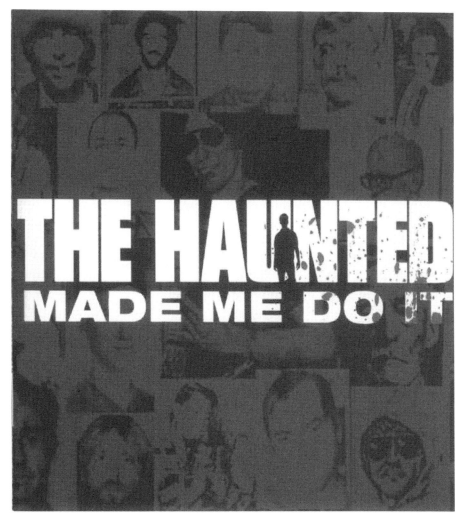

Richard featured on the front cover of The Haunted's 2000 album *Made Me Do It*, along with the likes of Albert Fish, Jeffrey Dahmer, Tex Watson, Columbine Killer - Eric Harris - and the Unabomber.

I was initially made aware of Rick's death from a friend who posted a link on my Facebook page. I recall being more surprised than saddened. I had no idea he had been battling B Cell Lymphoma cancer. His death went pretty much unnoticed by the Australian media.

Society will always judge him and understandably so. You really can't forget the innocent victims who met with terrible fates at his hands. He did, however, keep in touch with me all those years, and he did some genuine favours, such as send me what he could and looked out for chicks for me. What's that if it's not a friend? I don't, for one second, condone any of his crimes but I have to say, cheers for the friendship Rick.

The last mugshot taken of Richard Ramirez on San Quentin's Death Row in 2007.

Gallery

Artwork by Dan Boeren

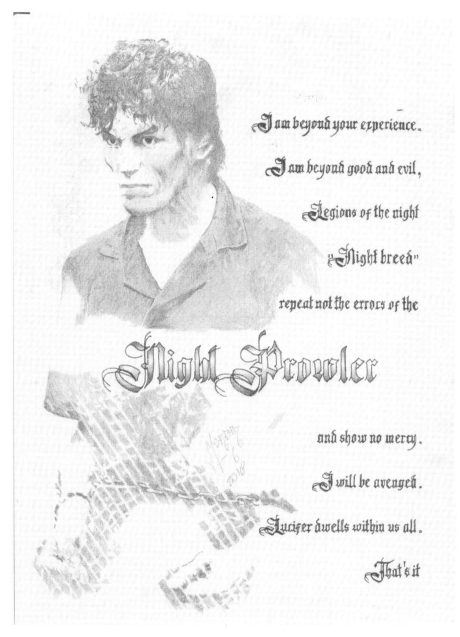

Artwork by Chad Morbid

Artwork by Chad Morbid

About The Author

Marquis H.K. is a self-taught independent writer and accomplished traveller. *Letters From The Night Stalker* - A Decade's Correspondence With Richard Ramirez is his fifth book. His other previous works include *The Sentinel Magazine* and *Slices Of Sin Erotic Comic Book*. He has been interviewed in various forms of the Australian media including Network Ten's *The Project* discussing the Black Arts and Satanism; he has been a member of the Church Of Satan since 2005. He also fronted Australian hardcore punk band Anger In Motion. His other passions include horror movies, dark and extreme music, as well as being an avid collector.

Other books by the Author

Thirty Years Of Anger

One Man's Journey Through The Australian Underground Hardcore Punk & Extreme Metal Scenes

An uncompromising, gritty and often brutal tale from someone who's lived this lifestyle firsthand.

Boolarong Press (Australia)

Frills and Thrills

A Fetishistic Celebration Of
Women's Sexy Underwear
and Lingerie

A fully illustrated celebration of all things sexy, saucy, sassy and naughty! From elegant silk suspender stockings and French knickers to sexy role play character costumes to comedy skits and celebrity wardrobe malfunctions. This is a sexy, classy publication that is sure to give you a thrill!

Eerie Planet

A Pictorial Study Of Some Of
The Darkest Places In History

A fully illustrated book that captures one man's experience at these places and what to expect if you dare to visit them. From the esoteric and paranormal to the lairs of historical tyrants.

Slices of Sin

An anthology graphic novel featuring four original titillating erotic tales

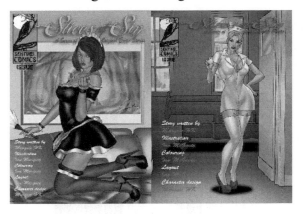

Featuring super hot French Maid Monique and Sexy Nurse Cassandra. Superb quality artwork.

Faces of Horror

A Lifetime of Inspiration
and Everlasting Impact

Presented here is a collection of films from a genre that has inspired the authors their entire lives. From classic Hammer Horror to 80s Slashers to real life hauntings and urban myths and legends.

$19.99

Letters From
The Night Stalker

A Decade's Correspondence

with Richard Ramirez

A first-hand account of the author's ten-year correspondence with one of the world's most infamous serial killers from San Quentin's Death Row. Packed with newspaper clippings, interviews, original artwork and letters and artwork from the killer himself!

$14.99

Printed in Great Britain
by Amazon